# Pastoral Ministry
# in Changing Times

*The Past, Present & Future of the Catholic Church in Ireland*

## Aidan Ryan

*Foreword by Bishop Colm O'Reilly*

ISBN 978 1 78812 082 1

Designed by Messenger Publications Design Department
Typeset in Times New Roman & Paciencia
Cover Image: iMoved Studio / Shutterstock
Printed by Hussar Books

Messenger Publications,
37 Lower Leeson Street, Dublin D02 W938
www.messenger.ie

# CONTENTS

# CONTENTS *Contd.*

# PREFACE

IT IS AN understatement to say that the years since the turn of the millennium have been a time of extraordinarily rapid change in Ireland. The rapidity and extent of change are without precedent in the history of our country. Change has affected all aspects of our society – our prosperity, our ethnic diversity, our lifestyles, our expectations and our attitudes to life and its purpose. All of this has posed massive challenges for Catholics and for people of faith in general. This book represents the efforts of one Irish pastor, ministering for these past twenty years in a rural midland parish, to understand and make sense of these changes. It is an attempt to find ways to think constructively about the challenges they bring and to address the questions they raise.

This collection had its origin in articles written for *The Furrow* magazine at various stages during the last twenty years or so. They were written on the invitation, and sometimes the insistence, of the late Fr Ronan Drury, a tireless promoter of reflection and debate on the Irish pastoral scene. This short book is a tribute of 'pietàs' to his memory. Because they were written over a period of years, inevitably there is some repetition, but then, perhaps some things are worth saying more than once.

If this book has a unifying theme, it is the idea of the ending of an era. The era now ending is described in this book, by way of a kind of shorthand summary, as the Cullen/McQuaid era, after the two towering archbishops of Dublin. Paul Cullen is generally regarded as the man who, more than any other, fashioned a particular type of Catholic life in Ireland after the Church emerged from the shadows of the Penal Laws. John Charles McQuaid, both in his episcopal style of governance and in his personality, can be seen as an embodiment of this style of Irish Catholic life at its zenith. This period is usually described by historians as post-Emancipation Catholicism. Whatever phrase one uses to describe it, it is obvious that this phase or era is coming to an end. The general thrust of these pages is an attempt to make sense of that ending, and to find some bearings in this transition time, with all its uncertainties and insecurities.

French scholars, commenting on this style of Catholic life fifty years ago or more, when it was still flourishing, coined the phrase 'catholicisme du type irlandais'. They saw this as marked by devotionalism, legalism, a certain tinge of Jansenism, an exceptionally high degree of religious observance, a high degree of deference to hierarchical personages and to clergy and religious generally and a weak intellectual life. Some of these features correspond largely with those named by Pope Francis as deviations from the Gospel message of Jesus, which he says calls us to a different set of priorities. How we can best find our way towards a new vision and towards the next era in the life of the Catholic community in Ireland is not at all clear at this transitional time. It will need a lot of reflection, dialogue and prayerful discernment to find the pathways along which God calls his people in Ireland at this juncture in our history. This book is offered as a modest contribution towards the ongoing search.

Aidan Ryan
*Ballinahown, Athlone*
*Easter 2019*

# FOREWORD

IT IS A privilege to have been invited to write a foreword to this collection of articles by Father Aidan Ryan. I am most pleased that Messenger Publications has given these reflections, originally published as articles in *The Furrow*, a more permanent format in a small book. This, I am happy to say, reflects the enduring value of these reflections for the life and mission of the Church as it travels into headwinds of new kinds and intensity in our time.

The first chapter takes us back to troubled times in the distant past, a reminder to us that the Church has had much experience of living with trouble. Indeed Church historians say that troubled times have been the norm, not the exception, in Irish history. The title of this chapter, 'The Last Monk of Clonmacnois', is highly evocative, focusing on the lonely figure of the last surviving monk after the final destruction of the great monastery as he celebrates Mass for the last time and blows out the last candle. He could have had dark thoughts about the future then. The metaphor is very apt for setting the scene for contrasting the fortunes of the Church from the destruction of 'St Ciaran's City Fair' to its present experience of keeping alive the wavering flame of faith.

In this chapter and Chapter 8, on the Catholic diversity in Ireland in the understanding of faith and its practice, we are offered an analysis of the state of the health of the Church in rural Ireland. Few writers from outside or inside the Church address in a measured way the flaws and defects in our communities and those charged with the task of leading them. Fr Aidan's lifetime of service in different pastoral ministries makes him well qualified to offer a balanced view of how the challenges of our time can be addressed by all in pastoral ministry. By giving examples of pastoral interaction he alerts us in a subtle way to how we convey messages about our values even in answering a phone call. On the positive side, I want to single out his hope for the Sacrament of Reconciliation being experienced as a sacrament of encouragement. He rightly begins his reflection on this subject by mentioning the fact that Pope Francis has placed mercy at the heart of the Gospel message, surely one of the great blessings for our time in the Church.

All of these pages contain both comfort and challenge. They will be helpful in stimulating reflection on how we can respond to the needs of a fast-changing society. They have the authenticity of being created from real experience and much thoughtful reflection.

I found most challenging the words that Fr Aidan put in the mouth of the last monk of Clonmacnois in his advice for our time from his perspective at the end of a different era. Here is a sentence from the monk as imagined by Fr Aidan: 'The prayers, or spirituality, or sense of God – that is the atmosphere which the Church breathes to live. Without it the Church suffocates.' I compare that advice, 'attributed' to a monk of the distant past, with advice given by Karl Rahner SJ with regard to a spirituality of the Church in the future. He famously said that Christians of the future would have to be mystics if they were to exist at all. He added that 'the ultimate conviction and decision of faith comes not from ... indoctrination but from the experience of God, of his Spirit ... bursting from the heart of human existence'.

The thoughts contained in this book are wide ranging but all point to trusting in the guiding hand of God. The poet Minnie Louise Haskins (1875–1957), in often quoted words, states the case for that reliance:

*Go into the darkness with your hand in the hand of God*
*That will be better than light and safer than a known way.*

+ Colm O'Reilly
*Bishop Emeritus of Ardagh and Clonmacnois*
*Deanscurragh, Longford*
*Easter 2019*

Part I:
Irish
Catholicism
Today

# CHAPTER I

## The Last Monk of Clonmacnois

THE ANCIENT monastic site of Clonmacnois is just a few miles from where I live. Sometimes, on long quiet summer evenings, after the visitors and tourists have gone, it is good to walk and pray among those ruins, to remember the glory days, when this was a thriving city, full of monks and scholars, and people came from all over Ireland, and from well beyond her shores, to drink at that great well of learning and holiness. That golden age lasted about 300 years from the time of St Ciaran. Sometime in the ninth century, the first Viking boat was seen coming up the Shannon to attack the monastery and steal its treasures. It was the beginning of the end for the great monastic city. It took several more centuries for the final end to come. Clomacnoise grew weaker and weaker as successive waves of destruction swept over it.

Walking through the ruins, my thoughts often turn to wondering about what it must have been like during those centuries of decline. What it was like at the very end, as the weakening monastic community of Clonmacnois lived out their days among the decaying ruins? In particular, what was it like to be the very last monk of Clonmacnois, the man who said the last mass there, and blew out the last candle? What would it be like to meet him and speak with him? What if we could tell him that after many centuries had come and gone, the Pope of Rome would come down from the sky in a red box and walk among those ruins, and speak to a crowd of 20,000 people? He would find it, no doubt, very hard to believe. And yet it happened.

What if that last monk of Clonmacnois were to come back and walk among us on pattern day for the feast of St Ciaran in September? He would immediately recognise the great sweep of the Shannon as it moves slowly and majestically through the Irish midlands, just as it did in his day. He would recognise the broad outline of the landscape. It might take him some time to recognise what was happening in the sanctuary. But he would notice that a book was being read and that the readings were being listened to with attention, and he would quickly realise that it was the same book, the same holy scriptures, that he and the monks copied and illuminated and read and studied all those centuries ago. He would see us take patens of bread and chalices of wine and bless and consecrate them and then share them. He would not understand the language and some of the gestures and ceremonies would be unfamiliar to him. But he would know that we were doing as he and his brethren had been doing, in a tradition handed on to them in the centuries that stretched back before their time to the upper room in Jerusalem.

He would know that we were doing what they so often did – fulfilling the command of Jesus to 'Do this in memory of me'. He would see that the four basic essentials of the Church were present – the brotherhood or community, the teaching of the apostles, especially as contained in the scriptures, the breaking of bread in the Eucharist, and prayer or a sense of God's presence. He would know that the faith that had come down the centuries before him had been passed on over the centuries that followed him, albeit in ways and forms that he could never have imagined.

There are questions we would like to ask that last monk of Clonmacnois. What was it like for him to live at the very end of an era? How did he manage to live a life of faith amid the decay and decline all around him? Was it difficult for him to see the very end of Clonmacnois as a living community of faith? Above all we would like to ask him what sustained him in that end-of-an-era time. We would be particularly interested in his answers, since we too live at the end of another era in Ireland. Given the prominence of Cardinal Paul Cullen in the shaping of the Church in recent Irish history it might be described as the era of 'Cullen Catholicism'. It has been an era of success and achievement – an era of full churches and full seminaries, with a priest (or several) for every parish, a convent (or several) in every town, an era when the Church enjoyed great prestige and status, and had a great influence all over the world, especially the English-speaking world, through the lives of Irish clergy, religious and laity.

My sense is that the last monk might say something like the following: 'It is very difficult to live through the end of an era, a time when "change and decay in all around I see" – a time such as yours, or mine. There is a huge temptation to discouragement or even to despair. It is a time of the testing of faith and trust in God. It is a time for going back to the basics – the core elements of what it means to be a follower of Jesus Christ.' These I take to be the four elements already mentioned, as stated in the Acts of the Apostles, that is the brotherhood or community, the teaching of the apostles or scripture, the breaking of bread or the Eucharist and the other sacraments as related to it, and the prayers, or a sense of God, a spirituality.

The community takes different forms down through the ages – sometimes large and powerful, sometimes small and weak. But the bonds of community, or communion, are what hold the Church together. The teaching of the apostles or the scriptures are always central – proclaimed and explained in the liturgy, pondered and prayed over in the hearts of believers. The breaking of bread, the Eucharist, the Mass, is the constant core of the Church in all its manifestations in history and all over the world. The prayers, or spirituality, or sense of God – this is the atmosphere which the Church breathes to live; without it, the Church suffocates. It is particularly important in difficult or transitional times to deepen one's sense of God's providential presence and care for his people in all the ups and downs of personal and communal history.

These thoughts and words would help me to return to my work and my vocation as a priest in early twenty-first century Ireland with a clearer focus on what I am about and what my priorities ought to be. They would give me a renewed consciousness of how the tides of history, like the tides of the ocean, rise and fall. Or to change the metaphor, the Church's pilgrimage through history encounters times of sunshine and times of storm, times when the going is smooth and times when it's rougher and tougher. Sometimes God's people travel through fertile fields and along shady forest paths, and sometimes through barren desert and windswept lonely moorland. At each phase in its journey through history the Church is called to the same basic essentials. However, differing circumstances call for different qualities and emphases, and each situation has its own temptations and challenges. In times of prosperity, the temptation is towards pride and arrogance. In times of adversity, it is towards cynicism and despair. All are to be noticed and resisted.

There are, no doubt, other figures in history who, like the last monk of Clonmacnois (who is, of course, more a symbol than an actual historical figure) and like us, lived at the end of their era, at times when what had seemed permanent and prosperous and pleasant was passing away, and there was no clear picture of the way ahead. What attitudes are called for then? What kind of spirituality can sustain us? Where can we find stories that will enlighten and guide us? Maybe one place is in the wilderness of Sinai. Perhaps ours is a time of exodus, when we are called away from the Egypt of our former securities, called to trust in God who leads us out into what seems a wilderness where there are no paths. (It is said that it took one day for God to get the Israelites out of Egypt, but it took him forty years to get Egypt out of the Israelites.) For all the faults we can now see so clearly about our Irish Catholic post-Emancipation period, which lasted well into the second half of the twentieth century, there was a certain security there that we still, at some level, long for. It will take a long time to leave that longing for security – for our 'Egypt' of success – completely behind, and move fully into the desert with trust and confidence in God who leads us forward into an unknown future towards a promised land we may not live to see.

Another place towards which we can look for lessons to learn is the backwater Galilean village of Nazareth. The lessons we can learn there are about simplicity, obscurity, distance from the corridors of power, lack of influence with the movers and shakers of this world. Perhaps the call of God for us at this time is a call to humility and littleness. Maybe we have been too arrogant, too confident in our own abilities to succeed, to make an impact, to make and mould our own future and our own Church. Maybe we need to learn again to be the handmaids/servants of the Lord, so that his plans for us, and not ours, may be fulfilled

So there are places that can teach us – scriptural places like the Sinai desert and Nazareth, local places like Clonmacnois, where the ruins remind us of the Celtic Church, or like Mellifont or Jerpoint, where the ruins recall the twelfth-century reform; and like the shrine of St Oliver Plunkett in Drogheda, which evokes the era of 'dungeon, fire and sword'. All these places have something to tell us about what lasts and what is merely passing. The question is – are we able to understand and to learn those lessons and to live by them?

So for us who live in an era of change for the Church in Europe and particularly here in Ireland, as the era of 'Cullen Catholicism' draws to a close, there are certain things we need to do. We need to face up to the fact that the tide is running strongly against faith – some have even described this tide as a tsunami – that it will not turn in any kind of foreseeable future, and that its destructive effects have not yet been fully seen. It has already swept away almost all the seminaries and many religious houses, as well as the numerical strength of the priesthood. It has decimated Ireland's long-term missionary presence in the developing world. It may well go on to sweep away some parishes and the presence of entire religious orders in Ireland. It will probably continue to sweep away the young, and even the middle aged and older, from regular weekly worship. It is in this situation that we are called to live and share our faith. Sharing faith is extremely difficult in the context of a culture such as ours which has become almost impervious to the Gospel, and threatens even our own faith. (It is said that we start out intending to convert the world, then would be satisfied if we could convert only a few, and end up being happy if we can prevent the world from converting us.)

The forces that destroyed Clonmacnois and its culture came in longboats up the Shannon. The forces that destroyed the 'Cullen Catholic' culture (along with much else in Ireland) have come in a much more subtle way, through channels of a different kind. The main channels have been various types of 'screen' – first large cinema screens, then small television screens, (later becoming larger) then computer and laptop screens, then smaller tablet and smartphone screens. Through these. for many decades now, a torrent of material has gushed into our homes, our public discourse, our minds and our culture, sweeping away so much of the past and filling every available space with a totally different way of understanding life and its purpose. Not all that comes in this way is bad. Some of it has been enriching, in a manner comparable to the positive elements brought into Irish life by the Viking settlements. But much of it, too, has been mind-numbing and desensitising and even dehumanising. In this new virtual world of fast-moving imagery, of superficiality and the cult of 'celebrity', of spin and manipulation, of crass consumerism and the dumbing down of the reflective faculty, there is little room for silence or for transcendence, for discernment or for the mystery at the heart of reality that Christians name as God.

In addition to these cultural forces in the wider world, there have of course been forces within the life of the Church itself which have contributed to the obscuring of the Gospel message. The most immediately obvious one has been the appalling abuse of children and young people by clergy and religious, and the prioritising of the Church's reputation over the pain and suffering of the victims. There has been the ongoing failure to reflect the dignity of women in the structures of Church life. There has been the alienation of some groups, for example divorced and remarried Catholics, who have felt condemned by the Church because of factors in their lives over which they have little or no choice. Decline and loss of influence cannot be attributed solely to external cultural factors.

Of course, the Spirit of God will still continue to move in human hearts, and those hearts will continue to have a thirst that only God can satisfy. There will continue to be the reflection of God, even if not explicitly recognised, in the work of artists and poets and reflective people of every race. The fruits of the Spirit – love, joy, peace, patience – will continue to be manifest in human lives. However, what is less than clear is the relationship that will exist between all this and the visible community of faith, and what form that will take in the future.

In this time of fast-fading cultural support for faith, we need to find, first of all, in small face-to-face communities or circles of friendship the support that faith needs – it has always been difficult to be a Christian in isolation, but today it is almost impossible. Some of the new movements in the Church may be able to provide this kind of community. It is difficult to see how an urban or even a rural parish, as at present organised, can do it, given the weakening of community, even in a secular sense, that is the consequence of the rise of individual choice. The kind of community people of faith will need in the future will involve some kind of intentionality and deliberate choice to belong, and a commitment to the other members that is based on more than a 'what's in this for me' mentality. There is little future, it seems, for 'faith communities' of mere social convention. These newer or renewed communities/circles will find in the scriptures, especially the gospels, the nourishment and guidance they need. They will need to have some kind of contemplative dimension, and they will need to celebrate the Eucharist together regularly.

While these communities of 'core' Catholics are forming and functioning, there will still be the wider circle of Catholics – traditional, creatures of habit, occasional churchgoers – who will expect 'their' Church to continue to provide the customary rites of passage – especially funerals and probably baptisms, some marriages, as well as first communion and confirmation while these sacraments continue to be linked to stages in primary school – though the faith content of these rites will be, in most cases, very little. Pastoral wisdom will be required to respond creatively to that reality, and to receive with kindness and welcome those requesting these rites. But even the best possible use of these occasions as opportunities to evangelise can expect little tangible result in the face of the subtle but profound influence of the prevailing culture on mindsets, mentalities and lifestyles.

So perhaps the last monk of Clonmacnois might focus his advice on the idea of communion or community. He might advise that newer, smaller and stronger forms of community and of communal faith-sharing should be sought and explored. He might suggest this not just as a pastoral or evangelising strategy but as a way for priests and people in this new 'diaspora' situation to find a way for their own faith to be sustained in a time when they might be tempted, as he himself may well have been, to pessimism and even despair about the future.

What kind of attitudes are helpful for people like that last monk of Clonmacnois, or ourselves who are the last generation of 'Cullen Catholics'? What qualities are fruitful and life-giving for people like him, or like us, who live at the end of an era? Could they perhaps include the following?

- Humility and simplicity, the ability to let go gracefully of positions of power and influence and the structure that re-inforces these, the ability to rely solely on the power of God and on the kind of influence that comes from lives lived with authenticity in the spirit of the Gospel.
- Trust and confidence in God, who leads his people in Ireland towards a future that we of this generation will not live to see, although we may glimpse some signs of the green shoots of a future harvest, and be able to nourish and water some of these fragile indications of future fruitfulness.

—  Joy and hope that flow from a deep personal awareness of the core truth of the Gospel – that we are God's beloved children, that our lives and our personal and communal futures are safely held in his hands and that there is no need to be afraid or despondent, however great the changes amid which we live.

—  An ability to share that core Gospel truth, not so much with words or structures or pastoral programmes, necessary and valuable as these may be, but by the quiet example of personalities that reflect Gospel attitudes, and lives that attract others by the way they witness to the goodness, compassion and love of God.

—  A preferential option for the least important, most marginalised and poorest – in both the material and spiritual sense, and an ability simply to be with them. To all who seem to be swept away from the Church and from the Gospel message by the tides of the prevailing culture, we need to show compassion, kindness and a friendly spirit.

—  A discerning spirit in facing the world, refusing simply to deplore and condemn, but seeking to find out how the Spirit of God may be at work in the currents of human history and in hearts of all people of good will.

Certainly the last monk of Clonmacnois has lessons to teach us. The question is – how best can we learn those lessons?

# CHAPTER 2

## At the End of an Era

ONE POSSIBLE way of understanding the history of the Christian faith in Ireland since the time of St Patrick is to envisage it as divided into eras – the brief Patrician period, the Celtic monastic era, the Anglo-Norman reformed Church, the Penal times, and the post-Emancipation Church. Each era had its strengths and weaknesses, and each era eventually ended. The latter era is sometimes called the Cullen Church, because of the dominance of Cardinal Paul Cullen in fashioning it. It could also be called the John Charles McQuaid Church, after its most representative figure. This is the era that is now obviously coming to a close. Or has it already come to a close? It may be helpful to reflect on how the Church in Ireland, and especially its ordained membership, is coping with this end-of-an-era time, on some of the questions this ending raises, and on what the future might hold.

When something ends – a human life, a community, or a particular form of Church life – there is a grieving process. People who study the grieving process – Elisabeth Kübler-Ross is probably the best known – note that there are a number of stages or strands in this process: denial, bargaining, anger, depression and, finally, acceptance. If one listens carefully to informal conversations in Church circles today, one can discern each one of these strands in the conversation of different individuals.

There are very few in denial, since the reality of something ending is so obvious for all to see. The bargaining is mostly retrospective and comes mainly in two forms, which could be described as from the right and from the left. From the right, it mainly takes this form: If only we had held on to the mystery of the Latin Mass and the clarity of the Maynooth catechism, and not compromised so much with the spirit of the age, then the era now ending could have lasted longer. From the left it mainly takes this form: If only we had made clerical celibacy optional, opened all levels of holy orders to women, given lay people a much greater say in doctrine and discipline, then we would have been able to negotiate our way much better through the recent and contemporary time of rapid social and cultural change. There is also what could be called a devotional form of bargaining – if only we had kept the family rosary going, if only we listened to what Our Lady has been saying in her various apparitions, then things would not have gone the way they have.

There is also an amount of free-floating anger around. It tends to focus mainly on two 'lightning rods' – the media and the bishops. It is undeniable that there is a clearly discernible hostility to religion in general and to Catholicism in particular in at least some sections of the Irish media. The anger directed at the bishops is mostly expressed through cynical comment, and is related to the retrospective bargaining outlined above and to the perceived failure of the bishops as a body to have taken whatever line – to the right or the left – is favoured by the individual who is in the 'anger' stage of the bereavement process. This is not to say that bishops, either individually, or collectively in the episcopal conference, are above and beyond criticism. There are those who would say that there are elements of dysfunction in episcopal ministry that need to be addressed. There are other objects of anger also – the priests and religious whose abuse did so much damage to children and young people, and to the Church, and the people who succumbed so easily to the blandishments of the consumer culture.

A further stage or strand in the grieving process is depression. Among the clergy, this can take the form of a pervasive mood of sadness and disappointment, and a certain withdrawal from the world as it is – a looking forward to (and planning for) early retirement, a certain sense of helplessness and an attitude of 'It will do for my time, it will see me out; after that, God alone knows what will happen.'

Finally, there is a an attitude of serene acceptance of the present Irish ecclesial reality as it is – a sense that this is our time, a time in which God asks us to be present as positively as we can, a sense that we are entering a new era in Ireland, an era that can truly be described as missionary. However, we have no training or expertise on how to be missionary in mentality, lifestyle or methodology. The challenge is to develop expertise, which is not easy for anyone, especially those of us in the evening time of life. We have been good at maintenance, which is about providing the sacraments and rituals and devotions of the Church for those who ask for them, as well as the buildings that are needed for this purpose. Mission is something very different and it is unfamiliar and uncharted territory for us.

One of the questions that often arises in the context of this grieving process is the question of why the Cullen/McQuaid era is now dying. Where did we go wrong? There are, no doubt, a multitude of reasons – massive, rapid cultural and social change, increased prosperity, the huge influence of mainstream and social media, immigration, travel. However, it is important also to acknowledge some major internal weaknesses in the form of Church life that is now fading. One is the excessive identification of Church people and Church life with the middle class in Irish society. The majority of clergy and religious come from that class, and the values we espouse are more those of Victorian respectability than of the Gospel. Our lifestyles are largely middle class – the houses we live in, the cars we drive, the holidays we take, the restaurants we eat in, the pastimes we engage in and even the political parties we tend to support. We have little passion for the travails that convulse the majority of our fellow human beings on this planet that is our common home. We have little anger about the gross injustice that condemns millions of our brothers and sisters to a life that fails to respect their human dignity. We are cosseted from worries about mortgages, family life, job insecurity. We have little of the hunger and thirst for what is right of which the Beatitudes speak. Many of us are personally generous, but not at any real cost to our comfortable lives. We are caught up in a merciless system and it does not bother us as it should. Our Church is too much like the society that surrounds it, and this society (to quote Pope Saint John Paul II) is taken up with the idolatry of money, ideology, power and technology.

At our clergy conferences (and even, perhaps, episcopal conferences) the topic that generates most interest, energy and passion is finance – far more than evangelisation, or social justice, or the sacredness of human life or the poisoning of the planet. We give the impression of being mainly in the business of maintenance and self-preservation. We are 'keeping the show on the road' without much reflection, it seems, on what the purpose of the 'show' is. We are largely a self-referential Church.

I recently heard a priest of my own generation, in a discussion of the present state of the Church in Ireland, say, 'This is not what we signed up for.' This provoked in my mind the uncomfortable question, 'What did we sign up for?' What did I sign up for when I went to the seminary in the autumn of the year of the JFK assassination (1963), and when I was ordained in the year of the first moon landing (1969)? No doubt we sincerely believed in the noble motives we professed – following Christ, bringing the Eucharist to the people, serving God. But is it possible that there were other less altruistic elements mixed into our motivation? Was there, perhaps, an element of signing up for a position of assured status in society, with housing and income, albeit modest, guaranteed for life, with little enough accountability for how we spent our time? Is it possible that some of the anger floating around is based on a sense of being robbed or cheated of that position of privilege and influence that went with the priesthood in the Church in which we were ordained all those decades ago? There is a further uncomfortable question that bothers me, by way of personal examination of conscience. Because of the material comfort of our lives and the relative absence of accountability, did we tend to become mediocre, even flabby, in our ministry? Did we tend, more and more, to 'do our own thing', to do only what we felt like doing, or even to do very little of anything? Given that we are more at home with maintenance than mission, is it possible that an undue amount of our declining energy has been devoted to the maintenance of our own comfort and convenience?

There are other internal features of the post-Emancipation Church that sowed the seeds of its own demise. One of the best speeches at the Second Vatican Council was made by Bishop Emil De Smedt of Bruges. He claimed that the three great sins of the Church were triumphalism, legalism and clericalism. There were plenty of all three in the post-Emancipation Church in Ireland. Most of the triumphalism has gone the way of the cappa magna and the ring-kissing. There is a greater awareness that laws are made for human beings, not vice versa. Clericalism is probably the slowest of the three to go, perhaps mainly because there are fewer clerics to maintain it, rather than because of any conviction about the need to move away from it. However, before these elements in the Church in Ireland faded, much of the damage was already done, as the sensus fidelium began to see more clearly how far they were from the teaching and example of Jesus of Nazareth.

So what will come next? What kind of Church will the next era see, after the now fading era has come to a complete end? It is never wise, or even possible, to predict the future, but some things at least can be said with some degree of confidence, and other things can be dreamed of with some degree of hope. It is clear that the Church of the future will be smaller, composed of intentional Catholics who have made a conscious option for Christ, for the values of the Gospel and for the community that proclaims and tries to live by these values. Its leadership will be quite different – it will be led, not by organisers or sacramentalisers, but by evangelisers, missionary disciples who have assimilated the Gospel deeply into their lives, who are passionate about it and have an ability to communicate it with enthusiasm. This leadership will be a mixture of male and female, and the question of who is ordained to preside at the Eucharist will be seen as of secondary importance. The primary question will be who can best proclaim the Gospel, firstly in his or her personality and lifestyle and then in the more verbal and visual forms of communication. This may be, in a strange way, a return to the first era, the Celtic Church. It is not clear if any or all of the major figures of that era – Finian, Enda, Ciaran, Kevin, Colmcille, even Brigid – were ordained or not, or ever presided at the Eucharist. What is important is that they were clearly seen to be people of the Gospel, with the ability to attract others to the following of Christ. Perhaps it is twenty-first-century equivalents of these who will lead the next era of the Christian pilgrimage in Ireland. Any renewal, at any time in the Church, always needs saints who will provide focus and inspiration and energy, which will renew the presence of Christ among his people.

A further feature of the Church of the next era will be a much greater involvement with people on the margins of society. It is significant that the face of the Church which seems most acceptable and respected in Irish society now is that embodied by people like Fr Peter McVerry, Sr Consilio and Sr Stanislaus Kennedy – all people who work with and for the broken and the wounded, and who seem to operate out of the 'field hospital' model of what the Church ought to be. Of course the post-Emancipation Church also cared for the poor and downtrodden – one has only to think of people like Edmund Rice and Catherine McCauley – but somehow what started out as a wish to respond to the poor in the spirit of the Gospel seemed to drift towards simply making the poor more respectable through an education that made them conforming and even successful subjects of a society that remained inherently unjust, turning them into fodder for the great consumerist culture that dominates our lives.

So where does all this leave us, the ageing last generation of Cullen/McQuaid Catholics and clergy? How can we live happily and constructively in this end-of-an-era time? What can sustain us in the in-between time as we await the coming of another era, whose contours we may vaguely discern, but whose flowering we probably will not live to see? A colleague recently said, 'I hope to spend whatever time is left to me doing as much good as I can, for as many as I can, for as long as I can' – not a bad ideal to set before oneself. We can continue to search for, and celebrate, those moments that invite people into something deeper than the soporific superficiality of the culture we inhale every day – moments like the wonder of new life in a family, moments of discovery of genuine love, even moments of darkness, death and bereavement. We can continue to invite people away from the tyranny of noise and haste that marks our times, and into the silence and stillness which is the language in which God speaks the message of abiding love to the human heart.

Perhaps we can learn lessons for our times from the saints of Ireland down through the centuries – John Sullivan, Catherine McAuley, Oliver Plunkett, Malachy the reformer, the great monastic saints, even Patrick himself. They would no doubt lead us even further back, to the earliest Christian communities and, ultimately, to the shores of the sea of Galillee, the upper room in Jerusalem and the road to Emmaus. In these places we have the best chance of glimpsing what God may have in store for his Son's disciples in Ireland in the time to come.

# CHAPTER 3

## Faith in the Future

IT IS COMMONPLACE now to say that the Catholic Church in Ireland is in crisis. It is equally common to refer to the fact that the Chinese character for 'crisis' indicates both danger and opportunity. There is a clear downward graph in many areas, including Mass attendance, finances, vocations to the priesthood and religious life, missionary enthusiasm and influence in the public square. Many of those who reflect on this reality would say that the basic issue underlying the crisis manifest in the various difficulties we are experiencing at present is the issue of faith. It is important to reflect on this issue and on how it might be addressed.

It is obviously important to be clear on what exactly we mean by the word 'faith'. We use it in a variety of ways, each of which emphasises one aspect of the reality of faith. For instance, those of us old enough to have learned the Maynooth catechism at school may remember the definition of faith as a 'divine virtue by which we believe and firmly accept the truths that God has revealed'. We learned an 'Act of Faith', which went, 'O my God, I believe in you and in all that you teach through your holy Church, because you have said it and your word is true.' The impression we got from all of this was that faith was something one did with the mind or intellect. It was an act by which one accepted as true certain propositions of doctrines far too deep and mysterious for the very limited human mind to understand – the Unity and Trinity of God, the Incarnation of Jesus as true God and true man, the resurrection of Jesus, the resurrection of the body, transubstantiation, the infallibility of the pope, to name a few. We accepted all of this on the authority of the Church, which we understood to be backed up by the ultimate and supreme authority of God. All of this was valid, and continues to be valid, as far as it went. But it needs to be supplemented by other understandings of the word 'faith'.

For example, if it is said of someone that 'she approached her death in a spirit of great faith', this not a statement about her acceptance of the truths revealed by God or about her capacity to say the Creed and mean it. It indicates, rather, a very strong sense of the presence within her of the personal and loving mystery at the heart of all reality that Christians name as God. It suggests a deep trust in the loving nearness of God and an ability to abandon herself completely into God's hands. This is faith as spirituality and as trust.

Another shade of meaning for the word faith is suggested by a statement such as, 'The Irish people are losing the faith.' What this is really describing is a loosening of the bonds that once existed between Irish people and the Church, particularly the Church's rituals, and especially the Sunday Mass. Practising one's faith mainly meant attending, from whatever motivation and with whatever level of participation, the weekly gathering of the 'faith community' in one's local church – or indeed in any church, where Mass was perhaps known to be shorter or where the time best suited your weekend schedule. What mattered was that you 'got Mass' and so could claim to be practising your faith. Thus, Christian faith can be understood as adherence to the Church, a sense of belonging, or at least a willingness to participate – even somewhat reluctantly – in the Church's rituals.

Of course, each of these descriptions has its own validity, and other aspects of faith would doubtless be needed to complete the picture. However, when one begins to consider how the faith might be shared, it is surely helpful to be clear on what exactly we wish to share, since the emphasis we place on one or other aspect of faith will certainly influence the ways in which we try to share it.

For instance, if we understand faith mainly as assent to revealed truth, then we will wish to communicate knowledge of the content of faith. We will encourage familiarity with the Catechism of the Catholic

Church. We will promote adult religious education. We will encourage an interest in the study of theology as 'faith seeking understanding'. We will try to preach doctrinally substantial and orthodox homilies. If our emphasis is on faith as an awareness of the reality of God, then our main focus in sharing it will be prayer and all that facilitates prayer – retreats, spiritual guidance, prayer groups, Christian mindfulness, Lectio Divina, the liturgy well celebrated (recalling the adage that 'good liturgy nourishes faith, bad liturgy damages it'). If our stress is on faith as belonging, then we will try to make our churches as welcoming as possible, we will emphasise outreach, we will try to use every opportunity, especially the sacramental moments of baptism, first communion, confirmation, marriage and funerals as opportunities to make and to strengthen connections between people and their local parish. All of these methods, with the underlying emphasis of each, are being used in Ireland today as part of our effort to share the faith with anyone who might be open to it.

It must be admitted, however, that even our best efforts seem to be bearing little enough by way of fruit. In thinking about why this is so, one area of reflection looms large. It is the area of culture. Like faith, the word 'culture' too can have a variety of shades of meaning, and be used in different ways in diverse contexts. For the purpose of this reflection, however, we may take it to mean something like the way people normally think and act and interact, the assumptions they hold in common, the things that influence daily life, 'the way we do things around here'. It seems clear that the difficulty with sharing the faith today in Ireland is very largely rooted in cultural change. It is a truism to say that, over the last fifty years or so, we have seen rapid and massive cultural change in Ireland, on a scale unprecedented at any period in our history. We have seen increased prosperity (albeit unevenly distributed), a huge increase in media penetration and influence, inward migration, much more frequent foreign travel by a much greater number of people. Our attitudes have been shaped by a much greater emphasis on the rights of the individual, and the idea of personal choice as the main criterion for morality. The idea of the common good has largely faded from our awareness. A consumerist approach to life has been very successfully promoted by huge marketing strategies, subtly but powerfully persuading us to want a multiplicity of things we don't need. Behind all this is the influence of western-style liberal capitalism, the supremacy of market forces, the 'throwaway culture' and the environmental damage that follows from this.

All of this is very different from the culture in which the Catholic faith seemed to thrive from the end of the Penal Laws until the last decades of the twentieth century. While it appeared that faith 'seemed' to thrive in that era, one could argue that many of the elements of faith were in fact much weaker than they appeared to be. In so far as assent to the truths revealed by God is concerned, Catholics of that era by and large believed them mostly in the sense that they did not deny them. In fact the average Catholic had, and has, little interest in doctrinal matters. As regards faith as a strong awareness of God, perhaps that was easier in a largely rural population, in tune with the rhythms of nature and ways of living that were much slower than the pace of life today. The two great enemies of awareness of God are noise and haste, whcich were largely absent from the culture of that time, and so a sense of spiritual reality came more easily. As regards attachment to the Church and its rituals, especially the Sunday Mass, one might wonder what motivated the extraordinarily high numbers of Sunday Mass-goers. It is undeniable that at least some of the motivation came from a strong sense of obligation and an even stronger sense of fear of mortal sin and the consequent danger of eternity in hell if one missed Mass deliberately without good cause. It is probably not unfair to say that the handing on of faith in that era had a large element of coercion built into it – believe this, do this, or else!

So where does that leave us now as the Cullen/McQuaid Church continues to decay all around us? Must we wait for it to disappear completely before it becomes possible to begin again from the ground up? There are those who would claim that the main difficulty about beginning again is the amount of energy that has to be expended on the quite substantial set of expectations that remain as a kind of legacy of the era that is ending: the continuing provision of sacramental rituals for people, for many of whom they are mostly social customs with little if any spiritual content; the ongoing involvement with an education network that in many instances is Catholic in name only, with the attendant stresses and pressures of increasing bureaucracy in this as in several other areas. All of this is simply 'keeping the show on the road'. It is maintenance rather than mission. Most of us, at least among the clergy, have been good at maintenance, we've done it well and have been happy doing it. But now we can see clearly that something else is needed. It makes sense to us that Ireland needs a new missionary impetus, but we don't know how to go about it. All our training has been for maintenance and we don't know how to go about mission in the new context in which we find ourselves, even if we had the energy and relative youth that would be needed for it. As priests become fewer and older, there will be even less time and energy available for anything other than maintenance.

However, a few things are clear about a new attempt to share the faith in Ireland. One is that we would have to be much more Christocentric (and maybe less ecclesiocentric) than in the past. At its heart, Christian faith can best be described as a way of looking at life and understanding it, a way of responding to life and living it, that is shaped and moulded by the teaching, example, death and resurrection of Jesus. Other aspects of faith – doctrine, awareness of God as loving father, a wish to share in the communal life of Jesus' disciples – all of these find their origin and focus in the message and person of Christ. In Ireland, there has been a tendency to see the Church as an end in itself, rather than as means to facilitate the encounter between the Risen Lord and his disciples. Perhaps we need to move the emphasis in the phrase 'People of God' from the first to the second noun in that phrase. It might also be helpful if we could rediscover the now somewhat forgotten theology of the Church as the Mystical Body of Christ. We would need to place the scriptures, and especially the Gospels, more clearly at the heart of our faith. The biblical apostolate would be pursued with more vigour and conviction. We would need to rediscover the beauty of Christ, especially as reflected in art and architecture. We would need to celebrate the liturgy in a way that mirrors both Christ's splendour and his simplicity.

There is much evidence to suggest that faith can only flourish in the setting of real community. In the context of the dominant culture of the West today, this community will need to be strong enough to be counter-cultural. It seems that faith tends to be stronger where Catholics are in a minority, and where such a status seems to produce a stronger sense of identity and sense of belonging to a faith community. Especially in mainland Europe, what are called ecclesial movements provide many with this communal sense of identity that supports an alternative way of looking at life, and living it, that runs counter in many respects to the mainstream ambient culture. In the past, this sense of community was usually provided by the local parish and neighbourhood. However, in the much more individualised (even atomised) culture of today, the parish, especially in urban areas, but in rural Ireland also, finds it more and more difficult to foster a genuine sense of community, especially in matters of faith. This may be linked to the tendency to see faith as mainly a personal and private matter, which most Irish Catholics are reluctant to display or even speak of in public. Attendance at Mass, for example, is often seen more as an exercise of individual devotion, or as doing one's religious duty than as a participation in communal liturgical worship. One task that a missionary project in Ireland might undertake would be to search for people who genuinely wish to see life, and live it, in a way that runs counter to the aggressive consumerism that constantly invades and pervades our lives. From among these it may be possible to form small communities that would try to be supportive of each other in tuning in to the Gospel and living by its vision and values.

A further feature of faith in the future would be an attempt to find points of contact with those features of contemporary culture that are open to the Gospel. Many of these are found in the Universal Declaration of Human Rights, which is an expression of a vision of human life on this planet that has much in common with the Gospel. Pope Francis has a great deal to teach us in this regard. His championing of care for the Earth as our common home is very much in tune with the concerns of thinking people today. His focus on the 'peripheries' and on those excluded from participation in a fair share of the world's resources is shared by the many people who work for greater justice for those who are the objects of discrimination and prejudice. His core value, which he describes with the word 'mercy', is surely shared by all who long for a more compassionate and inclusive society at every level. His emphasis on the family as the basic building block of society surely echoes the concerns of many people. In the future communities of faith would need to share all of these concerns, and small communities of faith would have to include commitment to all of these priorities.

There would be difficulties in the formation and life of such small communities of faith in the Ireland of the future. One such difficulty would be finding age and gender balance. Initially, older people would be more inclined to join, and women would probably join more quickly than men. Perhaps such groups might best be formed with young families, but including grandparents and the wider circle. Another difficulty might be differing theologies or styles of being Catholic – strong devotional enthusiasts and fervent social activists might find it difficult to cope with each other, while the doctrinally orthodox might have problems with the pastoral outreach of people with a more inclusive mentality. But as the history of the Church from the days of the apostles teaches us, there will always be differences and tensions, but ways can still be found to move forward together.

Another major difficulty would arise from the question of who would initiate and follow through on the formation of such groups.

It seems doubtful that such leaders/evangelisers will be found in families and parishes that are at present unable to foster vocations to the priesthood or religious life. It may well be that future renewal of this kind may have to come from beyond our shores, as it did in the great reform of the twelfth century when new orders like the Cistercians and the Augustinian Canons came from France at the invitation of people like St Malachy, to revitalise the weakening Church of that era.

We know that faith, both personal and communal, is ultimately a gift from God, and so we need to open our minds and hearts to the work of the Holy Spirit to discern what God is saying to us at this time regarding our faith in him and our feeble efforts to share it. The call of Pope Francis for a more synodical ethos in the life and leadership of the Church is gradually finding a response in the life of many Irish dioceses, by means of synods and assemblies and listening processes that strive to involve as many people as possible in thinking about and planning for the future. It is important that these initiatives be movements of genuine discernment, rather than mere exercises in the strategic management of diminishing resources. This ought to involve serious, genuine and sustained prayer on the part of all the participants. We need more than just the often perfunctory recitation of prayer formulas that sometimes begins Church-related meetings. We cannot deepen our faith or attempt to share it with others without an attentive listening for what God might be asking of us at this time. Discernment is not a familiar concept to many of us, or a skill at which we are proficient, but we surely need to learn it if we are to be guided by the Lord in the ways of faith, rather than simply trying to negotiate our way into an uncertain future relying solely on our own personal insights and our own very limited wisdom.

One of the great themes of the Hebrew scriptures is the theme of exile, especially arising out of the experience of those who were carried off into captivity in Babylon by King Nebuchadnezzar six centuries before the birth of Christ. The voice of Isaiah, as we hear it especially in Advent, was for them a message of hope and reassurance that, despite all appearances to the contrary, God had not forgotten his people. A parallel could be made for the community of the disciples of Jesus in many parts of the world today, not least in Ireland. We find ourselves living 'on alien soil'. We have hung up our harps by the rivers of the new Babylon that is, at least in part, the world we live in today We are finding it difficult, as the psalmist put it, ' to sing the song of the Lord in a strange land'. Yet this is our time and this is our place, and it is in this time and place that the Lord both consoles and challenges us in the living and sharing of our faith.

# Part II: Sacraments

# CHAPTER 4

## Going to Mass

It is obvious that there has been a great decline in regular Mass attendance in Ireland in recent decades. This is more marked in urban areas, but it is also a reality in rural parts. There can be few parishes in Ireland – at least in the Republic – where the rate is higher than thirty per cent of the Catholic population. It seems that Mass-goers are now a minority – albeit a large minority, in some parishes – of the overall Catholic population. What follows is an attempt to reflect on this reality from the standpoint of pastoral ministry in a rural midland parish.

Many factors have influenced the decline in regular Mass-going. One opinion is that it is largely to do with the fading of what were major motivating factors in the past – a sense of obligation, a fear of mortal sin and hell if one missed Mass, strong social and family pressure to attend, a widespread 'culture' of Mass-going accepted as the norm. The fading of these factors made more obvious the underlying weakness – or absence – of personal choice or motivation. Was almost universal Mass-going ever much more than a culturally conditioned phenomenon, which changed as the culture changed?

Combined with the fading of these cultural motivations, there was the rise of alternatives competing for people's time and interest – a lot of sporting activities on Sunday mornings and Saturday evenings, a much more active social life for many people, especially on Saturday evenings, with knock-on consequences for Sunday mornings. At first, people began to absent themselves from Mass only occasionally, but the occasions then grew more frequent until the habit was broken – Mass-going eventually became more and more the exception rather than the rule.

A Red C poll published some years ago in the *Irish Examiner* indicated that the principal reasons respondents gave – from a list of possible answers supplied – were mainly a perceived irrelevance of Sunday Mass to their lives, disappointment with the Church, particularly in relation to the scandals related to the abuse of children, a more individualised way of praying, and an honest admission of carelessness and even laziness. To these could be added the busyness of modern lifestyles, the fading of the idea of obligation (and even more so the idea of non-attendance as a sin) in relation to Sunday Mass.

It is relevant, too, to note the sectors of the population in which the incidence of occasionally attending families seems to be higher – urban dwellers, newcomers who have no roots in an area, and families largely dependent on social welfare benefits. In fact, this aspect of the question raises the issue of why participation in regular worship has become so markedly middle class in Ireland, and the related issue of the need to discern carefully between the values of middle-class respectability and the values of the Gospel. Even before the decline in Mass-going became widespread, the rate of Mass attendance in deprived areas – as in some parts of inner-city Dublin – was always low. Embarrassment about not being able to dress 'respectably' was one of the factors in these situations.

One anomaly regarding Mass-going is the increase, at least in some parishes, especially rural parishes, in requests for Mass to be offered for the deceased members of families. This has made it necessary, in some parishes, to celebrate what are called 'shared Masses', in which the deceased of a number of families are remembered. The attendance at these, depending on the size of the families concerned, can often be quite substantial, usually including quite a few people who are not weekly Mass-goers. If they are celebrated on a Sunday, they have a noticeable effect on the size of the congregation.

The general decline in Mass-going is particularly marked among younger people. This is also related to cultural change. Young people live in a world, a culture, a mental framework very different from that of their parents – even those parents who are not Mass-goers – a world centred on, and hugely influenced by, communications technology and social media – smartphones, the Internet, Facebook, Snapchat, Instagram, Twitter. Communication and even community is virtual, and face-to-face interaction, apart from work and sport, often takes place in environments dominated by alcohol and the possibility of drug-taking. Mass-going is utterly foreign to this way of living and relating to others.

Where people continue to attend Mass, their motivation is often a kind of residue or remnant of the older culture – hence the predominance of older people at most Sunday Masses. Where there are younger people attending, there is often an element of family tradition strong enough, at least for the present, to counter the cultural drift away from Mass-going. No doubt there is a deeper motivation in some people – a genuine thought-out commitment to faith and to all that nourishes it, a reflected-upon deliberate decision to be a regular worshipper. Such people are in a minority, however.

One of the things that strikes observers is the relative passivity of Mass-goers in Ireland – in contrast even with our neighbours in the UK – manifested as a reluctance to move from the back half of the church, to sing or even to join in the responses. There are, no doubt, historical reasons for this, but it seems to represent real failure in our efforts to renew the liturgy since the Second Vatican Council. We have invested a great deal of effort – and money – in renewing churches as spaces for worship. We have worked hard – and with some success – with choirs and church music, with the liturgical ministries of readers, ministers of the Eucharist, altar servers etc. Thought and effort have gone into the roles of presider and homilist. However, a major element – the assembly, the worshipping community, the congregation – has largely remained passive, despite our best efforts at congregational singing, provision of texts etc. The majority of Irish worshippers seem to approach the Mass as a kind of exercise of private, personal devotion, with little sense of connection to other worshippers except perhaps momentarily at the sign of peace. Their participation is individualistic and devotional, much more than it is communitarian and liturgical. Why this should be so in a more marked way in Ireland – as distinct even from other countries with a large Irish element in the Catholic population, for example the UK, Australia, the US – is difficult to understand.

Some questions might be asked regarding a possible link between a decline in attendance and the quality of our celebrations. For a priest simply to attend Sunday Mass, perhaps while on holiday, as a member of the congregation in the back half of the church, can be an eye-opening experience, certainly very different from the experience of Mass as a presider. Are there too many Masses, resulting in small congregations scattered through a space too large, and a very diminished sense of community? Do an excessive number and frequency of Masses result in an over-familiarity, both for the priests and for the people? Does a proliferation of Masses diminish appreciation of the Eucharist? Is the Mass experienced as a torrent of words, perhaps recited rapidly and without much obvious conviction or sense of being in the presence of the numinous, the transcendent, the Holy One? Or is it experienced as a folksy but false attempt by a priest to jolly people along with 'entertaining' or even 'pious' personal interjections into the liturgy?

What do people really hope for, deep down, when they come to Mass? A nourishing, uplifting experience of spiritual reality? A celebration that is marked by dignity, solemnity, some silence and reflection? An oasis of calm in a busy, even stressful, week? And what of the Liturgy of the Word? Is the diet too rich – or too wordy – for the average congregation? Are three readings too many, or might two, proclaimed and preached well, be better? Are homilies sufficiently affirmative and encouraging – a naming of grace – or are they bland and insufficiently challenging?

What is the likely future of Mass-going in Ireland? Has the decline 'bottomed out' or will it continue? There are at least two possible scenarios. The first is 'worst case' – exemplified by the situation in some parts of rural France, where the percentage of Mass-goers is in single figures, with the vast majority of those tiny congregations ministered to by an elderly priest with more than a dozen churches in his pastoral area. A 'better case' scenario also envisages smaller Sunday congregations, but with a good balance of age and gender and social background, made up of people and families who have consciously committed themselves to the Catholic faith and to active participation in worship and the life of the local Catholic community – people who could be described as 'intentional' Catholics, as distinct from 'cultural' Catholics. A major task for the Church in the coming years will be the promotion of 'intentional' Catholicism. This will involve finding new ways to present the Gospel message in a manner that is attractive to people, 'to lead people into an appreciation of the beauty of friendship with Jesus', as Pope Benedict might phrase it.

And how do we do that? This question brings us back to the basic issue of motivation – how do we motivate people towards a conscious positive option for faith, for the faith community and for worship?

In our own parish we try to keep the following motivations for weekly worship before people, for example in the parish newsletter and in homilies:

- Jesus invites me – 'Do this in memory of me'
- The community needs the support of my presence
- My faith needs the support of a believing community
- The Gospel can challenge me
- The Bread of Life can nourish and strengthen me
- Weekly Mass anchors my week and my life
- God has blessed me, so I give thanks
- I have needs, so I ask for God's help
- Worship combats spiritual laziness
- Worship give depth, direction and meaning to life

These presentations of possible motivations for Mass-going may help some people to continue to worship regularly, or to take up the practice again. But a wider and deeper response to the issue seems to point in the general direction of evangelisation and adult faith development. The blueprint for this in Ireland at present is *Share the Good News* (2010). Despite the initial publicity at the time of its publication, this document seems to have slipped well down the agenda of the Church in Ireland since then. In any case it is not a 'quick fix'. I suspect the solution may be very much about the long haul of addressing basic issues of faith – how it begins, how it does or does not develop, what diminishes it, what nourishes it. These are crucially important questions for all serious Christians in Ireland at this time.

# CHAPTER 5

## Going to Confession

DURING THE Year of Mercy in 2015 we were invited to consider all the ways in which the mercy of God is communicated in the world. Mercy, as we have learned more clearly from the teaching and example of Pope Francis, is at the very heart of the Gospel message. It is an attitude, a mentality, even a lifestyle, that is characterised by compassion for the human condition in all its woundedness and weakness, by a capacity to accept people where they are without condemnation, by a willingness to forgive and be reconciled and by an instinct to reach out to those on the edge, on peripheries of any sort, in an inclusive and welcoming way.

Among the ways in which the Church tries to communicate the mercy of God is the Sacrament of Reconciliation, previously known as the sacrament of penance. How might this sacrament best be understood and celebrated in a way that most effectively communicates, in our current cultural circumstances, the forgiveness, mercy and love of God for human beings in their weakness and their inherited tendency to turn or drift away from the friendship which God so much desires to share with his people? It might be helpful to look at the history of the sacrament.

For the first five centuries confession was a very public event involving sinners who had been excluded from the gatherings of the Christian community because of some serious sin, such as murder, adultery, worship of pagan gods. Having repented, and confessed their sins to the bishop and undertaken a period of public penance these penitents were publicly welcomed back by the bishop into the Christian community in joyful liturgy of reconciliation.

In the period after Constantine this public confession was replaced by the practice of private confession to a wise monk, who advised and prescribed penance, but may not have granted absolution (most monks were not ordained priests). In 1215 the Fourth Lateran Council decreed that Christians should confess their mortal sins to their parish priest at least once a year.

After the Reformation the Tridentine definition of the sacraments included penance, confessionals were installed in churches and the requirement to confess the number and species of our sins was introduced.

Later, as a result of the establishment of sodalities that encouraged frequent confession and communion confession became more frequent. The first half of the twentieth century was marked by a dramatic increase in the frequency of confession for the average Catholic, linked to the encouragement of frequent communion. Recent decades have seen an equally dramatic decrease in the number of Catholics going to confession regularly, if at all.

Why have confessions diminished so dramatically? The first answer one often hears when this question is discussed is the loss of the sense of sin. I'm not so sure about that – surely one can only have a sense of sin if there is first of all a sense of grace in its broadest sense, a sense of the goodness and love of God that evokes a deep and habitual gratitude? A sense of sin is simply an awareness of having failed to respond to this. A colleague expresses this with the homely analogy of potholes – a pothole, he says, is not a thing in itself, it is simply the absence of road where road should be. In a similar way, sin is not a reality in itself but the absence of grace where grace should be. Perhaps what has been lost is not so much a sense of sin as a sense of guilt, and that might not always necessarily be a bad thing, as when it leads to an unhealthy scrupulosity. For many ordinary Catholics, one suspects, the ordinary small failures of life in areas such as impatience, custody of the tongue, sexual (= 'bad') thoughts, failing to find time for personal prayer – do not really count as sins at all, or if they do they are merely venial and do not necessitate going to confession. There is the related dissatisfaction with a ritual recital of these same peccadilloes in frequent confession, a kind of sense of pointlessness in 'going through the motions' over and over again. A further contributory factor to the decline of confession is the contemporary cultural stress on the fundamental equality of all human beings, and in a Christian context, the equality before God of all the baptised. This leads to a questioning of why it is necessary to confess to another human being. The modern person tends to give more emphasis to the person of the priest than to his role as a mediator of God's mercy, and to question such mediation more than a person used to a more hierarchical culture might do.

Underlying all of this is the question of how widespread deliberate personal alienation from God is in the world and in the local church. The key word here is 'deliberate'. It is abundantly clear that there is a widespread cultural alienation from God. God is missing, but not missed. This has an effect on the majority of Catholics, who tend, as do most people, to go with the cultural flow. The element of personal choice, which is an intrinsic part of personal sin, seems to be largely missing.

All of this raises the question of how the mercy and compassion of God can best be celebrated sacramentally in the context and culture of our times. Certainly, Pope Francis has enthusiastically promoted the traditional form, both by his teaching and by his personal example. The pastoral initiative of 'Hours for the Lord' halfway through Lent has met with a good response in some places and has potential for growth.

The Church requires as essential only the confession of serious/mortal sin. Most ordinary Catholics, most of the time, do not commit mortal sin in which all three conditions are present – grave matter, full knowledge and full consent. Therefore most Catholics, most of the time, are not bound to go to confession. This does not in any way devalue the practice of going to confession, but is it true that most of the confessions that were heard in the days of larger numbers and greater frequency were in fact what could be described as confessions of devotion, rather than what might be called confessions of necessity? It is arguably somewhat inaccurate to describe such sacramental encounters in terms of reconciliation, since there was no real prior alienation from God.

On the other hand, it could be argued that all of us who suffer from the effects of original sin are in some sense and to some degree alienated from God. In this perspective, the regular confession of venial sins is part of a lifelong process of conversion, a constant – even if gradual and uneven – turning of our lives away from selfishness and towards God. Regular confession – even of venial sins – can provide a salutary opportunity to review our lives and perhaps to identify areas of moral 'slippage' before they become more serious. The biblical adage 'He that contemneth small things shall fall by little and little' (Eccles 19:1) still has validity. Regular confession can serve as kind of spiritual check-up, analogous to the regular physical check-up so frequently recommended by doctors.

Perhaps this is why Pope Francis places such emphasis on confession, hearing confessions during most of his pastoral visits, and very publicly approaching the sacrament himself during penance services in Rome. In the first interview he gave after his election, he was asked, 'Who is Jorge Mario Bergoglio?' After a long pause he answered 'I am a sinner'. What exactly did he mean by that? Did he mean 'as a young Jesuit provincial I made some mistakes that with hindsight I regret'; or ' as a human being, I am enmeshed in a world order that is a net or web of sinfulness that oppresses the poor, insults human dignity and is progressively poisoning the planet'; or ' I could try harder not to fall asleep when I pray in the late evening, I could be more patient in my thoughts about those who frustrate or annoy me, I should fast more than I do'? These three expressions of sinfulness – which could be replicated in the lives of most Catholics – will obviously influence our understanding and practice of confession.

Confession of devotion has a great potential for good if we can envisage it differently, not only as forgiveness of sins, but as a source of encouragement and as a simple form of personal spiritual direction. People always need encouragement and will welcome it. Many people would welcome spiritual guidance and reassurance regarding their status as the beloved children of God. But this would involve a significant change of mindset on the part of most priests and lay people who celebrate the sacrament as a confession of devotion. Rather than an emphasis on failure, however little or great, there would need to be an attempt to clarify how the 'penitent' – if that is the appropriate word in this context – understands him/herself in relation to God, how deeply the Gospel message of God's infinite love and compassion has penetrated into the heart and soul, and how it might be enriched by a deeper experience of prayer. The emphasis would move from guilt to gratitude and from vices to virtues and values. The sacrament could be described as a sacrament of affirmation and encouragement, a sacrament of guidance and spiritual direction, at least as much as a sacrament of reconciliation. The emphasis would be more on growth in loving and being loved by God than on the elimination of imperfections and the many minor lapses that mark the human condition as lived in daily life. While there certainly are imperfections and lapses in every human life, the language of 'striving for perfection' is less attractive to the modern ear than the language of 'doing the best I can', or 'realising my potential for spiritual growth'.

In the average Catholic parish in Ireland now – certainly in rural parishes – the main way in which the sacrament of penance is celebrated is in the form of an adapted version of Rite II, usually celebrated in Advent and Lent. The celebration is communal in character, with those participating coming forward to a priest to whom they either mention one specific area of their lives or simply make a general admission of sinfulness and a request for God's mercy and forgiveness. The priest gives individual absolution and a penance and the rite ends with a communal thanksgiving. Some describe this – perhaps disparagingly – as 'Rite Two and a Half'. There are some who are unhappy with this, because they feel it goes beyond what the rite envisages and lacks sufficient emphasis on the need to name sins by number and species. However, it seems to make the mercy of God more accessible to many, including to some who have not been inside a confessional for many years. One has the impression that most of those who participate in services of this kind are seeking not so much reconciliation with God – from whom they do not in any case feel alienated – but a blessing on their lives or some type of healing or encouragement; what they sometimes describe as 'the grace of the sacrament'. Many of the participants are elderly and what they are often seeking is reassurance regarding remnants of guilt that still remain with them from the preaching and teaching of the culture of the Church in which they grew up, particularly in the area of sexuality. These services seem to be effective in communicating the mercy of God, as expounded particularly by Pope Francis.

Regarding those in a more real and serious situation of alienation from God through life-styles and attitudes at variance with the call of the Gospel, the call to repentance still needs to be addressed in a challenging yet compassionate manner. Opportunities should be provided – perhaps especially in places where many people go on pilgrimage or in city centre churches where there is a large passing 'footfall'. The pastoral initiative of having priests available in shopping centres has much to recommend it here. Priests who are gifted with an ability to welcome, to rejoice with and to encourage, can be found who would enter, in such places, into a 'waiting' ministry, inspired by the mentality and spirituality of the father of the prodigal son.

Mercy, compassion, forgiveness – these, as Pope Francis consistently reminds us, are at the heart of the Gospel. One of the ways in which the Lord wishes to communicate these to the wounded and the lost is through the sacrament of reconciliation. The challenge of our time is to find ways to unblock whatever may have been impeding the flow of his loving welcome through this sacramental channel, so that the heavenly rejoicing over even one repentant sinner may continue in our time.

# CHAPTER 6

## 'Occasional' Catholics and the Sacraments

ONE OF THE pastoral problems facing the Church in Ireland is the question of how to respond to requests for the sacraments – baptism, first confession and communion, confirmation and marriage – from families where there is a very low or non-existent level of religious practice, understood as regular attendance at Sunday Mass. The expression 'non-practice' is often used to describe this reality, but this term has limitations, since 'practice' can cover anything from mere physical presence inside the church door (or even outside it), combined with a morally questionable lifestyle, to full, conscious and active participation in the liturgy, combined with a lifestyle marked by the fruits of the Holy Spirit. Perhaps a more helpful term in discussing the underlying pastoral challenge might be the term 'occasional' Catholic, understood as those who come for special occasions – Christmas, maybe Easter, weddings and funerals, baptisms, confirmations, first communions, family anniversaries etc.

There is a temptation to be negative or condemnatory towards people who have drifted away from Mass-going. This may be particularly the case when they come to a priest wishing to have a child baptised, or their marriage celebrated in church, despite being rarely, if ever, present at weekend Mass. They are, by and large, good and decent people with a positive attitude towards the Church and they consider themselves Catholics. Some of the opinions they may express relating to the Church are often simply an unreflective mirroring of what is coming at them strongly in the media, but they have not, in any real sense, rejected faith or Church membership. Some, indeed, have a level of reflectiveness and interiority that suggests an underlying spirituality. But many have simply drifted away from Mass-going, carried along in that direction by the general drift of the culture that surrounds them, in a manner similar to the way that many of their forebears were carried by a cultural tide towards Mass-going by the very different culture in which they lived in their time. Most people are much more influenced by the prevailing culture (or sub-culture) in which they live than they are aware of or would be prepared to admit. To impute bad faith, disloyalty or hypocrisy to those who have drifted would be unfair, judgemental and pastorally unhelpful. Laziness there may be, and a certain lack of depth, but the attitude of the one who 'had compassion on the multitude because they were like sheep without a shepherd' is surely more appropriate in this situation.

One wonders to what extent it may be true to say that for the majority of Irish people, Mass attendance has always been largely a matter of social conformity. Most people tend to go with the cultural flow and to take their cue regarding appropriate behaviour from those around them. When the cultural flow was towards Mass-going, most people went with that flow. Now that the cultural tide has turned, and is now away from Mass-going, many people go with that flow too. The high levels of practice in the past may not have indicated high levels of commitment, and the lower levels of today may not indicate a corresponding rejection of the Church or the Gospel message. Even those who rarely attend Sunday Mass are very keen to mark important moments of their lives with Catholic rituals. Most of these would be quite offended by any suggestion that they were less than fully Catholic.

Many, if challenged, will say that even though they are not regular Mass-goers, they lead good lives – some will even claim, and not without justification, that they lead better lives than some Mass-goers. This raises the underlying theological issue of the relationship of the Church to the kingdom of God, and whether it is more important to live by Gospel values – either consciously or implicitly – than to participate in religious ritual. The scriptures seem clearly in favour of the former. Of course, it is not an either/or choice. Participation in the Eucharist ought to bear fruit in Gospel living.

What is the best way for the Church to face the issue of requests for sacraments from 'occasionally' attending families? By way of initial response, it seems important to recognise the need, especially for priests, to avoid two extremes. Firstly, there is the confrontational approach, which may come from respect for the sacraments, but could come from a personality trait that is aggressive or controlling. This may be seen by the priest concerned as challenging, as the Gospel challenges. Secondly, there is the easy and accommodating laissez-faire approach, which may come from a sensitivity to people and a reluctance to alienate them, but could also come from a personality trait that is conflict avoiding, needing popularity and being well thought-of. This may be seen by the priest concerned as a pastoral or compassionate approach, mirroring the pastoral compassion of Christ. Either of these factors or personality traits may be at work in a subconscious way in a priest, of which the priest himself is largely oblivious, although it is perhaps obvious to others. Midway between these extremes there is an approach that might described as dialogical, persuasive, invitational and pastorally creative.

Some years ago, at a clergy conference in our diocese, we had a talk from a speaker who outlined the four stages of evangelisation using the Greek words used in the New Testament – *koinonia, diakonia, kerygma* and *eucharistia*. He explained that these words mean that we begin by establishing and maintaining good human relationships with those we wish to evangelise, then we respond to their needs (as they, not we, perceive them), then in some way we share the Jesus story with them and, finally, we help them to recognise him in the breaking of bread. Many of our pastoral problems, the speaker suggested, arise from expecting people to be at stage four (*eucharistia*), without our having led them through the other three stages first. In the past, when the sense of community was much stronger and when catechesis was more intensive, much of the earlier part of the process could be presumed. That is not the case now.

So how, at a practical level, do we approach requests for sacraments from 'occasionally' attending families? It seems to me that we should begin with the general attitude of using such requests as an opportunity to engage in some aspect of the evangelising process. This is an area to which we need to give a lot more thought – what exactly is meant by evangelisation, especially in an Irish context? What are its content, its aims, its methods? How is its effectiveness assessed or judged? In particular, what kind of attitudes and mindsets are needed for evangelisers in Ireland now? For years we have been hearing about the need to move from maintenance to mission, but what exactly does that mean in practice? What steps can we take in that direction, especially those of us who are priests in parishes, and so deeply enmeshed by training and tradition and expectation, and sometimes even by aptitude and preference, in the work of maintenance in its various aspects and levels?

It may well be that we have much to learn from other countries which have coped over a longer period with the changes in the religious landscape that have swept so rapidly over Ireland in recent decades. What can we learn, as regards the preparation and celebration of the sacraments from the experience in most of mainland Europe, and the wider anglophone world? Who might research for us the experience of how others before us have coped pastorally with the process of secularisation? How might such research, if carried out, help us to frame our responses to what, for us, is a fairly new situation?

If we regard requests for sacraments from 'occasionally' Catholic families as an opportunity to engage in an evangelisation process, a few thoughts occur. With regard to baptism, it ought to be diocesan policy that every parish, or every cluster of parishes should provide a baptism preparation programme, which should ideally include a visit to the home by a priest or, in large parishes, by another representative of the parish, and a meeting of about one hour's duration in which the ceremony of baptism is explained, and its implications for the child and for the family clearly spelled out. Attendance at this meeting should become as accepted a part of preparing for baptism as pre-marriage courses are for marriage. Care would be needed to make the meeting as friendly and as non-threatening as possible for parents, a genuine expression of the phrase in the baptismal rite – 'The Christian community welcomes you with great joy'. If it is seen as just another 'hoop' through which parents must jump so that their child can be baptised, then it it will not achieve very much. Welcome is a key theme in the baptismal liturgy, as it is a key theme in evangelisation, and so it seems reasonable to hope that it will be part of the preparation process also.

With regard to confirmation, many people think that the time has come to consider detaching the sacrament from the school situation, and making it a parish and family responsibility. There are radical voices which would argue in two opposite directions. Those who view the sacrament as part of Christian initiation would have it celebrated in conjunction with baptism (as it was in the early Church and even today in the Eastern Churches), or perhaps with first communion. Those who view the sacrament as one of maturity and commitment would argue for the age being raised, perhaps to sixteen, eighteen or twenty-one. Since both of these views are too radical to have any chance of acceptance in Ireland in the foreseeable future, perhaps consideration might be given to moving the celebration by just one or two years into the time of early second-level schooling. Young people, having studied the sacrament as at present in primary school, would be invited to attend perhaps four or five gatherings during the year in the parish (or cluster), of a catechetical and/or liturgical nature, and would also be required to show some level of commitment to Mass-going and to church involvement during the year. Such a change would need careful long-term planning and would need to be flagged, especially to parents, at least four or five years in advance, for example at the time of the young person's first communion. There would need to be consideration of where, when and how the sacrament might be celebrated, and the provision of parish-based catechesis would of course provide its own challenges. However, it seems clear that to continue with the present situation in which confirmation is a 'sacrament of exit' for so many young people, detached from any expectation of involvement in the worship and life of the faith community, is pastorally unsustainable in the long term.

All baptised Catholics have a right, and, indeed, an obligation, to have their marriage sacramentally celebrated in a church, even if they normally have little or no contact with a worshipping community. Therefore, there can be no question of denying the sacrament of marriage to a baptised person who requests it and is canonically free to marry. However, the practice of almost always celebrating the sacrament in the context of the Mass is highly questionable. It ought to become normal practice, when a couple come to arrange their marriage, to put to them the possibility of celebrating it in the context of a prayer service rather than a Mass, and to point out the inappropriateness – not to use a stronger word, such as insincerity or even hypocrisy – of people who are not Mass-goers 'going through the motions' of attending Mass and even receiving the Eucharist (probably under both species), simply because they think it is the norm, and is expected of them. Putting this issue in a pastorally sensitive way to couples when they begin to prepare their marriage ceremony may be a good way to raise with them the issues that can so easily be glossed over when answering the question in the pre-nuptial enquiry form regarding religious faith and the resolve to practise it regularly.

Perhaps the most difficult problem in the whole area of sacraments and non-practising families is the question of first communion and the associated celebration of first confession. Here the connection be-tween school and sacrament is most deeply entrenched, and the sight of whole classes of children, especially girls in their white dresses, is an integral part of the early summer in Ireland. It sounds a deep chord in the Irish psyche, mostly because it is a celebration of childhood and innocence. To tamper with any aspect of this – for example by suggesting that it be celebrated, not in class groups, but by families on a day of their own choosing – is likely to meet with a great deal of resistance. To suggest that children be denied this once-off celebration simply because of non-participation in the life of a worshipping community, would surely be perceived as punitive and harsh.

So, how can we best respond to the non-practising family that wishes their child to receive first communion? A significant step forward in this area in recent years has been the widespread use of the *Do this in Memory* programme, initiated in 2005. The invitation to families to participate at least monthly in the parish Mass during the year prior to first communion is a gentle invitation to them to come more often. The effort to involve the home as well as the school and parish in the preparation is surely a step forward. At this point, after some years of use, it would be helpful to conduct some kind of survey to see how this programme has worked in the different kinds of parishes in which it has been used. It might then be possible to modify and/or improve it in the light of what is now a very wide experience. A much more radical possibility would be some form of return to the pre-Pius X practice of beginning to receive the Eucharist at a later age, perhaps linking it with confirmation and thus restoring the original order of the sacraments of initiation.

One thing that seems clear regarding those sacraments that are school-related, is the importance of the process of enrolment at the beginning of the school year. This is a privileged time for putting to families the need for Sunday Mass attendance and prayer at home, to back up the preparations being made in school, and to suggest to them the hollowness of celebrations that have no background of faith or prayer.

It is highly desirable that the initial enrolment be followed by the rest of the *Do this in Memory* programme for prospective first communicants. For candidates for confirmation in the present school-related arrangement, it would seem important that they have some kind of ongoing involvement in church life during the school year – serving at Mass, singing in a choir, reading prayers of the faithful. There are ceremonies linked with confirmation – the ceremony of light, a commitment ceremony and perhaps a pledge with regard to alcohol/drugs – which seem at present mostly to be held in the weeks leading up to confirmation. It might be better to have these spread throughout the year – perhaps having at least one of them in early February or pre-Lent – so that the occasion could be used to stress again the basic need for Sunday Mass and prayer at home as a minimum preparation for a genuine celebration of confirmation as a significant moment in the faith-life of a young person.

These sacramental moments are all moments of pastoral opportunity. A central underlying idea is the concept of community, or *communio*, or *koinonia*. The challenge is to use these moments in a way that invites people gently and perhaps slowly and gradually a little deeper into *communio* than they now are.

The fundamental attitude of the priest is enormously important in this process. Individuals or families who request a sacrament may sometimes appear to him to be careless, blasé or sometimes even lacking in basic courtesy. But the pastoral challenge is to see beyond that 'front' to the human reality that lies behind it. A confrontational or adversarial approach will almost always be counter-productive. That is not to say that people should not be challenged. But the pastoral task is to do the challenging in a way that will not be read as a 'put-down' or as lack of sensitivity to individuals and to their life situations.

Some people, despite our best pastoral efforts, will never be regular Mass-goers. It is still important to approach the celebration of sacraments with such people in a way that is a good experience for them of that involvement, transitory though it may be, in the life of the Church. Practice, understood mainly as attendance at Sunday Mass, either before or after the celebration of sacraments, ought not to be the only criterion by which the celebration is judged.

The quintessential pastoral qualities of charity, patience and compassion, as well as imagination, creativity and persistence, are needed in addressing these issues. In trying to bring these qualities to bear on the issue of 'occasional' Catholics and the sacraments, the priest and the parish community models this ministry on that of the Good Shepherd, who promised to 'look for the lost one, bandage the wounded and make the weak strong'.

# Part III:
# Parish
# Life

# CHAPTER 7

## Pastoral Priorities

NEARLY FIFTY years ago, when the late Cardinal Cahal Daly was a young bishop in Longford, he was asked what he found most difficult about being a bishop. His memorable reply, phrased, one suspects, with tongue in cheek, was, 'My most difficult task is that of prioritising among the plurality of my competing commitments.' Many priests could identify with that, since our life is often a jumble of diverse tasks, the urgent often taking the place of the important, and the sacred frequently mixed with the banal. So it can be good, sometimes, to step back a little and look at our lives and to sort out, at least for ourselves, what our priorities are, or at least ought to be. This reflection is an attempt to do just that, from the personal and limited perspective of one parish priest in a rural parish with three churches, four primary schools and two priests.

My top priority, the most important thing I do, is the preparation and celebration of the Eucharist, particularly Sunday Mass, which in my own circumstances, I celebrate three times most weekends, twice in the parish church and once in another church. Preparation is the key to celebrating well, and it includes a number of elements. First among these is my personal prayer life. I don't pray primarily to prepare for Sunday Mass – prayer would be necessary even if I never celebrated Mass – but to be in touch with God, trying to go deeper into the heart of reality, trying to see beyond the daily urgencies into the dimension of transcendence. All of this is important, even essential, if I am to celebrate the Sunday Eucharist reverently and prayerfully. If I don't pray outside the Mass, I won't pray within it. I'll just be mouthing words, reading a rather empty formula, and somehow the people will pick that up. So to prepare for Mass, I need to pray, or at least I need to try to pray and to keep trying.

More remote preparation for Sunday Mass includes the whole business of church maintenance – ensuring that the buildings are in good condition, well heated and lit, with a good sound system. It includes the recruiting and training of readers, ministers of the Eucharist and altar servers, and the encouragement of choirs and of some congregational singing. It includes the provision of worthy altar furnishings, sacred vessels and vestments. It includes all the elements that help to create an atmosphere of welcome, joy and prayerfulness. Candles and lights, flowers and icons, liturgical decor that reflects the seasons are all important. Increasingly, some of these latter aspects are being looked after by finance committees and liturgy groups, but these groups too need recruiting, guidance and encouragement, and this in turn takes time and effort. All of this, as I see it, is included in making the celebration of the Sunday Eucharist not just my personal first priority, but that of the parish also.

My second priority, obviously linked to the first, is the preaching of the Word of God. Here, too, prayer has an important place. Before one can preach well, one must ponder. One must read and reread the Word of God during the week, if one is to share it effectively at the weekend. Commentaries and even sample homilies are useful, but to preach convincingly I must have made the Word my own in some way. It has been said that for each minute one preaches, one should spend an hour in preparation. That would probably be unrealistic for most pastors – half an hour per minute might be more realistic. The homily ought to be high enough on our list of priorities to warrant that kind of expenditure of time. In addition to his role as presider and homilist, the priest is also present as pastor. This aspect of ministry is more directly expressed in the priest's interaction with people before and after Mass, and this may be, at least for some worshippers, a very significant part of the experience of going to Mass.

My third priority is involvement in primary schools. This has to do, to some extent, with natural inclination and aptitude. Ever since my first appointment as diocesan catechetical adviser for primary schools,

I have always felt at home in the classrooms and staffrooms of primary schools. The *Do This in Memory* programme for children preparing for first communion, and our own parish adaptation of it to include pupils preparing for confirmation, is something I believe deserves a high priority in the expenditure of time and energy. It puts us in contact, eventually, with nearly all the Catholic families in our parish, including those who are not churchgoers, and puts before them in a non-threatening way the invitation to be participating members in our worshipping community. Even apart from sacramental preparation, a priest's regular presence in a school puts him in touch with families he might rarely meet otherwise. His seemingly inconsequential chatting with children about the latest school sporting triumph or disaster, or the smaller ones' news about the tooth that fell out, the cat that died or the cousin that was born, ensures that at least his name is a household word in the children's homes. Teachers are enormously influential people in the lives of children, and any effort we can make to be supportive of their positive presence – and not just catechetically – is well worth the time and energy involved.

Another aspect of involvement with primary schools is chairing boards of management. This, I feel, is better done, if at all possible, by a lay person with managerial skills, if an appropriate person can be found to undertake the task. This does not mean that the priest abdicates responsibility for the school. Ideally, the priest should be the patron's second nominee, should be there as supporter and encourager of the lay chairperson, and should represent the specifically religious and spiritual aspect of the entire educational project. However, in practice, for a variety of reasons it is often necessary for a priest to take on the role of chair of the board, and the tasks associated with that role. Sometimes, especially if there is a building project, or staff appointments, or difficulties within the school, the priest's time and energy is taken up with these, to the detriment of his pastoral presence among the pupils and teachers. In these circumstances he can just do the best he can, while hoping and, if possible, planning for the day when he can find someone better to do this job, enabling him to give the priority he wishes to the pastoral, catechetical and pre-sacramental work of the school.

My fourth priority is the preparation and celebration of important sacramental moments. This overlaps to some extent, with the previous priority, which included preparation for first confession/communion and confirmation. The other key moments when a priest is in touch with people – often with people who are not Mass-goers – is on the occasion of baptism, marriage and funerals. There is a school of thought among some clergy that maintains that we ought to be much more challenging than we are when people come to us regarding these celebrations, especially the first two. There is some validity, I think, to this, but it is very important to challenge in a manner that is not negative or judgemental. Faith, among its other attributes, is an invitational reality, and part of our role as priests is to invite people gently into a way of thinking about these key moments that is attractive and life-enhancing. Many people, despite our best pastoral efforts, will never be regular Mass-goers, but that does not mean that our pastoral efforts are a failure. If people experience the pre-baptismal visit to their home or their participation in a pre-baptismal meeting as a real expression of care for them and their new baby, and if in the baptismal liturgy they are able to celebrate the birth of their child as a gift from God, then somehow the Gospel touches their lives. If they experience the pre-marriage interviews with the priest as a friendly and respectful dialogue, and if they are enabled to pledge their love to each other in a ceremony that is dignified and prayerful, then something of Christ's presence comes into their lives. If they are enabled to mark the passing of someone dear to them in a manner that is grateful for, and respectful of, both the life of the deceased and the faith of the Church, then something of the Christian message about the dignity of each person and about eternal life is communicated. People request the sacraments from a mixture of motives, but somewhere in the mix the Spirit of God is at work. As

Pope Francis says, the desire for a sacrament is itself a gift from God.

It would be a mistake to judge these sacramental celebrations solely on whether or not they are preceded by, and lead to, religious practice. Ideally, of course, they should, but if people's experience of the Church on these occasions is of a welcoming and respectful community, then something of the Gospel message has reached them.

My fifth priority is the pastoral care of the sick and, more generally, of those who are distressed or in difficulty of any kind. This priority finds its most regular expression in the monthly First Friday calls to the homes of the sick and housebound, and in visits to hospitals and nursing homes. Also in need of special pastoral care are people suffering from bereavement, or coping with loss of any kind, especially the loss of a spouse through separation or divorce. More irregular are the conversations with people who come looking for prayers to be said, or Masses to be offered for a variety of intentions, or who are seeking advice or just a listening ear.

These top five priorities absorb, I estimate, about two thirds of my time and energy, and I am happy with this – I think that is more or less as it should be. The problem begins to arise in relation to about ten other areas on the pastoral agenda, and the manner in which they compete for space, time and energy in the time and energy that are left. These areas include, in no particular order, the following:

- **Lay involvement in pastoral and finance councils** – while convinced of the value of these, one can find that recruiting, electing, training and encouraging them can be more time- and energy-consuming than doing things oneself, a temptation to be resisted

- **Home visitation** – everyone seems to agree that this is important, despite the increasing difficulty of finding a suitable time to call

- **Pastoral contact with teenagers and young adults** – perhaps via involvement with youth groups, e.g. Foróige, or visiting the various secondary schools

- **Transparency and accountability with regard to parish finances**
- **Implementing child-protection policies**
- **Promoting vocations**
- **Promoting mission awareness and practical support for missionaries**
- **The ministry of reconciliation** – penance services in the parish churches and in schools, regular availability for confessions
- **Promoting temperance regarding alcohol and abstinence from illegal drugs** – if these are major threats to our young people, our parish life should mirror our concern for them
- **Eucharistic and Marian devotion** – pilgrimages, patterns, prayer groups
- **Promoting justice in the world via Fair Trade and Trócaire**
- **Pastoral care of immigrants and emigrants**

With regard to any one of these, there are people who can make a good case that a particular area should be at, or near, the top of our agenda. But, obviously not everything can be first, or even second, priority. Some of them are more important than others, and the relative importance given to them will vary from one priest, or one parish, or one time of year, to another. But none of them can be totally absent from our agenda – hence the need for some kind of sorting out of priorities if we are not to become first disoriented and then discouraged when trying to keep all the bases covered, and all expectations met.

Hence the wisdom of Bishop Cahal Daly's insight all those years ago – the difficulty and yet the need to prioritise among the plurality of our competing commitments. It is something that we need to do regularly – to stand back a little to see the wood for the trees and to discern how best to invest our limited time and energies, which grow more limited with the passing of the years.

# CHAPTER 8

## Catholic Diversity

IN EVERY parish in Ireland there are a variety of Catholics and a variety of ways in which they interact with their pastors. The following are a few representatives of that variety, followed by a small sample of pastoral interactions, and a reflection on what might underlie them.

Nora is a nominal Catholic. Her parents were not very enthusiastic about their religion either, but they had her baptised, because that was the 'done thing' at that time. They sent her to a Catholic primary school, mostly because there was no real alternative locally, and there she 'made' her first communion and her confirmation, but since then has had little or no contact with the Church. Nora is passionate about justice in the world and about the future of the planet. She is an active member of Amnesty and of Greenpeace. In the census form in 2016, she ticked the 'Catholic' box, mainly because she considered the alternatives even less appropriate to describe her religious situation.

Oliver is an occasional Catholic, in the sense that he attends church or worship for particular occasions – Christmas, funerals, weddings, christenings, Cemetery Sunday and the anniversary Mass he has offered for his parents each year. His main expectation of the Church (never consciously articulated) is that it will provide a ritual framework for moments of significance and transition in his life and in the life of his family. He is actively involved in his local community as a trainer of under-age teams and as secretary of his local Tidy Towns committee. He has no awareness of any link between what happens in churches and what he sees as 'real life'.

Patricia is a practising Catholic. She attends Mass most Sundays, without thinking very much about it. If she were asked why she attends Mass she would probably say that was a habit she got into from her youth, it was what her parents brought her up to do, and because she was taught that it was her duty or obligation to go. She works as an special needs adviser in her local school and is greatly liked by the children and the school staff. She sometimes prays during the week, but mostly she just gets on with the business of living without making much connection between Mass-going and daily life.

Conor is a committed Catholic. For a number of years in his teens and young adult life he abandoned the practice of Mass-going that was the norm in the family in which he grew up. When he married, and especially when his first child was born, he began to see a need for some kind of framework to guide his life, to be a source and support of his values, and the need to have some kind of 'bigger picture' to balance what he began to see as the pervasive consumerism of the culture. At a certain stage, he made a deliberate choice to be a Catholic. He is a member of the local conference of the St Vincent de Paul Society, attending a meeting and visiting the poor every week . At weekly Mass, he tries to take something from the Word of God to think about during the week, and he hopes the homily will be helpful.

Dorothy is a devout Catholic. She goes to Mass not only on Sundays, but often on weekdays as well. She says the rosary most days and goes to Knock a few times each year. When there is a funeral or wake in her area, she is among the first to come with a tray of sandwiches and is behind the scenes making tea in the kitchen for those who call to sympathise. She is a kindly person, a good neighbour, a positive presence in the circle of her friends. Her faith life is centred on the rituals and traditions of Catholicism.

George is a Gospel Catholic. He was always a practising Catholic, somewhat like Patricia above, but he had a kind of conversion experience at retreat some years ago and subsequently joined a prayer group which is based on a prayerful reading of the Gospels. He regards the person of Jesus as the centre of his life. He is a volunteer with a local group that helps people with disabilities, especially children, and travels with them to Lourdes for a week every Easter.

Of course there are other kinds of Catholic too – the crusading Catholic, the critical Catholic, the cultural Catholic, the theologically informed Catholic – to suggest only a few. And few Catholics fit completely and neatly into only one type – many are some combination of two or more types. All of this adds up to a great variety and diversity in the Catholic population of most parishes.

Let us imagine that the first two, Nora and Oliver, who are in a relationship, have a child whom they wish to have baptised. They telephone their local parish priest. There are two extremes in the kind of reception they might experience:

## Scenario One

**Nora:** Father, I want to talk to you about having my child christened.

**Fr Stan Osborne** (of the Strict Observance party): Do I know you? Are you a Mass-goer at our church?

**Nora:** No, Father. I haven't been to Mass in a long time.

**Fr Stan:** Well, come to Mass here next Sunday, and meet me afterwards in the sacristy. If I see you at Mass here every Sunday for the next three months, then we can begin to talk about christening your child. See you on Sunday.

**Nora:** Thank you, Father.

## Scenario Two

**Oliver:** Father, I want to arrange to have my child christened at your church.

**Fr Adrian Gannon** (of the Anything Goes party): We have Baptisms here on the last Saturday of every month at two o'clock. Bring two godparents, a candle and a white shawl. And of course, don't forget the child.

**Oliver:** Thank you, Father. See you on Saturday week.

As it happens, Patricia and Conor, who are married to each other, also have a child for baptism. When they contact the priest, they are invited to attend a pre-baptism meeting in the local parish centre. The meeting is conducted by the local priest, who leads it, and the parish sister who gives the input on the ceremony and the significance of its various parts. In introducing the meeting, the priest spends a long time chatting with the gathering of couples, and the individual parents who are there. One couple has brought their baby, and the priest spends a lot of time admiring the baby boy, and talking about the mystery of new life. Then he asks the parents present about their babies, their place in the family, the difference they make to the couples' lives, their names and why they chose them. The atmosphere grows warmer and more relaxed.

Meanwhile, the parish sister, who is a teacher who took early retirement, is wondering will she ever get to give her carefully prepared and very clear presentation of the ceremonies of baptism and their meaning. Eventually, she does, using PowerPoint, a clip from a DVD and a summary page which she distributes at the end. The meeting ends with a short prayer service led by the priest.

Afterwards, when the parents have left, the priest and the sister, who work well together, discuss the meeting. The sister asks if all that chat at in the early part of the meeting was really necessary or if the limited time could have been more effectively used for more catechesis and information for the parents. The priest observes that baptism is all about welcome and that it is actually better to welcome people than just to talk about it.

Meanwhile, back at home, over a cup of tea with the babysitting granny, Conor and Patricia also discuss the meeting. Conor particularly liked the clarity of the sister's presentation, and thought the priest waffled a bit in the early part of the meeting. Patricia said she most enjoyed meeting the other parents and hearing about their babies, and thought the sister was a bit 'teacher-y'.

Dorothy and George are mother and son. They have a difference of opinion related to the forthcoming baptism of Dorothy's first grandchild, George's baby daughter. The difference is related, not to the baptism itself, but to the choice of godparents for the baby. George wishes to ask a couple who are good friends of his and who are heavily involved in the local Simon community. However, they are not Mass-goers, and Dorothy has a difficulty with this. She feels it is asking them to be dishonest when asked, during the ceremony, to help the parents bring their child up in the practice of the faith, since they are not practising themselves. George feel that they would be good role models for the child in practical Christian discipleship. He can support his viewpoint with several biblical quotes – 'What I want is love, not sacrifice'; 'Faith without good works is dead'; Matthew's 'These people honour me with their lips, but their hearts are far from me'; Micah's 'This is what Yahweh asks of you, only this' etc. They consult their local priest, Fr Matt O'Roarke (of the Middle of the Road party). He suggests that only one of the Simon community couple be invited to be sponsor and that another – Mass-going – sponsor be added. He presents this as a compromise, but both Dorothy and George consider it to be something of a fudge.

Underlying the interactions just described there is a tension that has marked the Church since its beginning. It is sometimes described, especially in the media, as the liberal/conservative divide, with the liberal side usually portrayed in a better light. One wonders how the term 'conservative' has become so pejorative at a time when 'conservation' in all its forms is viewed with favour. Many would feel that these labels are inadequate and misleading in describing the varieties of approach to the life of the Church.

Perhaps it might be more helpful to think in terms of what one might call the 'Petrine' and the 'Pauline' principles inherent in the nature of the Church. The 'Petrine' principle is the one that calls the Church to be true to its origins, to hold firmly and courageously to the truth of the Gospels, to teach and apply those truths through its Magisterium, to be faithful to its millennial traditions, to maintain the bonds of communion across the continents and across the centuries. It is significant that the ministry of the bishop of Rome is described as the Petrine ministry.

The 'Pauline' principle is the one that sends the Church ever outwards in fulfilment of its missionary mandate, to every time and culture across the globe, meeting people where they are and attempting, with them, to inculturate the Gospel in new times and new situations. This principle is always seeking new ways to communicate the Gospel message and to enter into dialogue with the great diversity of cultural milieus, attempting to discern the movements of the Spirit of God by an attentive reading of 'the signs of the times'. It is striking how much this principle seems to be at work in the ministry of Pope Francis.

A moment's reflection will show that both of these principles must be at work in the life of the Church, in respectful dialogue and sometimes in creative tension with one another. If the 'Petrine' principle predominates excessively, the Church risks becoming atrophied and stunted, self-referential and inward looking. If the 'Pauline' principle predominates excessively, the Church risks dissolving into the general culture and splintering into a collection of sects.

To return from this broader picture to the particularities described earlier – what does this broader picture say to the scenarios outlined there, especially to the priests of the various 'parties' involved? To some extent, individual personality styles enter here. Some people are by nature idealistic and challenging, others tend to be more realistic and indulgent towards human weakness. Pastoral ministry is always filtered through human personalities, but it is important that people are not simply subjected to the whims and personal preferences of individual priests. Hence the importance of agreed norms and policies for the interface between the variety of types of Catholic and the variety of pastors with whom they interact. The danger with such norms and policies, however, is that they might be implemented in a rigid and legalistic kind of way, or even used as a kind of blunt instrument to bludgeon unconventional Catholics into submission. On the other hand, the absence of such norms and policies may subject people to interactions with priests that may seem to be 'pastoral' and 'caring', but are in reality based on a desire to avoid conflict or unpopularity at any cost, and a reluctance to make the effort to establish relationships in which the challenges of the Gospel can be more easily understood and accepted.

The Petrine/Pauline tension runs right through the history of the Church from New Testament times. It continues today in contexts as varied as ecumenical councils and synods to the nitty-gritty encounters of everyday parish life. The important thing is to keep the tension creative rather than destructive, and to keep the dialogue ongoing, charitable and mutually respectful.

# CHAPTER 9

## Liturgy in Ireland Today

On 4 December 1963 the first decree of the Second Vatican Council, *Sacrosanctum Concilium*, dealing with the renewal of the Church's liturgy, was officially promulgated by Pope Paul VI in St Peter's Basilica. I was at the time a first-year seminarian at the Irish College in Rome and had managed, with a fellow student, to infiltrate myself into the ranks of the Sistine Choir as it entered the basilica. Thus I found myself for the duration of the ceremony, beside the statue of St Peter, opposite the cardinals, for the promulgation of the decree, and for the announcement by Pope Paul VI that he intended to visit the Holy Land, the first pope to do so since St Peter.

In the years that followed, as seminarians, we saw the reforms coming in stages, with the vernacular introduced in March 1965, and concelebration the following year. In 1968 we were among last cohort in the Church to receive the sub-diaconate before that order was abolished, and the next year we were among the first to be ordained to the priesthood using the revised rite of ordination. As young priests we saw the introduction of the revised rites for the other sacraments, and began to pray the new Breviary in the vernacular. We lived those years, one might say, on the very cusp of change.

A lot of water has flowed under the bridges of the Tiber since those far-off days, so it is good to pause and to reflect on the experience of how *Sacrosanctum Concilium* has been implemented, especially here in Ireland, with particular reference to the Sunday Mass. The first thing that strikes one is how enormously different the celebration of Mass is now as compared with the previous era. The use of the vernacular has replaced the universal use of Latin. The position of the priest vis-à-vis the congregation has subtly but deeply influenced the dynamics of the gathering. The fussy rubrics have been replaced by a noble simplicity. There is far more lay involvement through the ministries of readers and of the Eucharist. Choirs have a much more varied repertoire. People have become more familiar with a greater variety of scripture passages.

An immense amount of time, thought, effort and money has been expended on liturgical renewal. The work of the Irish Liturgy Institute has been most impressive, as has the work of the Irish Church Music Association. This has been replicated on a more local scale in liturgy commissions/committees in dioceses and parishes all over the country and has found expression in many folk groups and choirs of various kinds. Many millions of pounds, punts and euros have been spent on the renewal and redesigning of churches and sanctuaries to provide a more fitting setting for the liturgy as envisaged by the Council and to promote the work of Irish architects, artists and craftspeople. All of these advances flow from that decree of 4 December 1963. They are real graces given to the Church.

However, it seem to me that there is one crucially important area where the work of liturgical renewal is still meeting with subtle but stiff resistance – at least in Ireland – and that is in the area of 'full, conscious and active participation' by the most fundamental and basic element in the liturgy, the worshipping congregation.

Having spent almost thirty years as a pastor in two rural parishes, I have the clear impression that somewhere in the Irish soul, at a level well below conscious awareness, there is a real resistance on the part of the average member of the average congregation, to active participation in the liturgy. There is a desire to observe rather than to take part, a wish to remain passive rather than to be active. This shows itself in a reluctance to participate in congregational singing or even in the responses and prayers proper to the congregation. The recent introduction of a new Missal, with the literal translation of Latin prayers, has surely not helped. The body language of wishing to be seated (or even to stand) near the back of the church, as the majority do, speaks volumes about interior attitudes. It shows itself in phrases like 'getting Mass' and in the desire for a 'fast Mass'. Very little of this is at a conscious level – it is something much deeper, in the psyche or the soul of the average Irish worshipper and the average Irish congregation, and is therefore very difficult to address. Words, explanations, exhortations, catechesis – all these can address the conscious mind, but that is not, in my view, where the difficulty lies.

No doubt, there are historical reasons for this reluctance to engage, and for the tendency to approach liturgy in an individualistic and devotional frame of mind rather than as a communitarian act of worship. Historians and social psychologists may be able help us understand how Irish Catholics came to have these attitudes towards liturgy, and in particular to the Sunday Eucharist.

Perhaps part of the reason may be found in the 'devotional revolution' associated with Cardinal Paul Cullen in mid nineteenth-century Ireland. Largely due to his influence, and the influence of religious orders giving parish missions, devotions that had not previously been a prominent part of Irish Catholic spirituality were promoted in Irish parishes – devotion to the Sacred Heart, to the passion of Jesus, to Mary as queen and mother, to the worship of the Eucharist outside Mass and, indeed, to regular attendance at Mass on weekdays. Since many of these devotions were more individual and personal than communal expressions of faith, they may have contributed to a kind of privatisation of spirituality that carried over into liturgy. Even today, many people would find it difficult to see or to articulate any difference between attendance at weekday Mass and at Sunday Mass, and would tend to approach both mostly as devotional exercises.

Of course, devotional exercises continue to have (or ought to have) a role in the prayer-life of Christian communities. For example, the ceremony of Benediction, with its candles and incense and its familiar chants, so similar in several ways to the Taizé style of prayer, still has a great appeal for many people, despite that fact that is now a much rarer experience in Irish parishes. Similarly, the continuing popularity of novenas such as those in Galway or Limerick and several other places has something important to tell us about how the Irish soul is nourished by devotions that touch the heart. The fact that at these devotions people seem more willing to sing, and even to occupy seats towards the front of the church, raises questions about elements that may be lacking in the more formal structure of the Mass.

The resistance to communal participation at Mass, which is deep in the Irish soul, is not evident to anything like the same extent in other countries and cultures. A constant refrain from Irish missionaries returning from abroad, and from Catholic immigrants coming among us, is how dull and lifeless most of our liturgies – especially our average Sunday liturgies – seem by comparison with their experience elsewhere.

As well as this resistance to participation, there is another area where the Vatican Council has left us – and not only in Ireland – a somewhat ambivalent legacy. It is the area that is known as the '*ars celebrandi*'. In the post-conciliar liturgy, the personality of the celebrant is a much more prominent element in its celebration, especially the Mass. For those of us who may have a subconscious need to draw attention to ourselves, the role of celebrant offers a subtle temptation to do just that, for example by playing the chat-show host or the entertainer or by substantially altering the prayers and rituals of the Mass. For those of us who tend towards loquaciousness, the Mass offers an opportunity (inadvertently) to drown the congregation in words – of introductions to the penitential rite and to the readings, the interpolation of personal pieties after communion, and extensive remarks at the end of Mass, not to speak of the possibility of a lengthy rambling homily. It is certainly possible – and indeed desirable – to preside without being intrusive and to be prayerful without being overly pious, but this is an art to be learned and a skill to be acquired, and our training for this has been scant. It is possible to preside without dominating and to lead worship with dignity and with minimum intrusion of our own personalities. There are many celebrants who do preside with dignity, with a simple style and quality of presence. There is ample anecdotal evidence, however, to suggest that some celebrants still have a lot of learning to do in this regard. Some would suggest that in most of our churches the sanctuary area can have the appearance of a theatrical set and this may subconsciously influence some celebrants to 'act a part' or even to be theatrical in their manner of presiding. The assembly is then subtly reduced to the role of audience, and the most that can be hoped for is 'audience participation', which is surely far short of what the Vatican Council envisaged.

Another area worthy of mention in the context of liturgical renewal is the persistence of the practice of distributing communion from ciboria kept in the tabernacle. When we do this, we are ignoring the exhortation, not just of the conciliar documents, but of a succession of popes from as far back as Benedict XIV in the eighteenth century, that people should normally receive the Eucharist with hosts consecrated at the Mass they are attending. The underlying theology is the notion of the Eucharist as a shared sacrificial meal. To use a banal analogy, communicating people from the tabernacle could be compared to inviting people to dinner and then giving them yesterday's (or even last week's) food from the fridge. Some priests have an understandable fear of running out of hosts, but surely it is not necessary to pack the tabernacle with several full ciboria. Most worshippers, of course, don't even notice this practice, but that is not a good reason to continue it.

There is one liturgical area that seems to have a particular resonance in the Irish psyche and that is in the area of the rituals that surround death. Funerals and evening removals are probably the best attended liturgies in many parishes and the celebration of an annual Mass in cemeteries brings what may well be the largest congregation in the parish in the course of the year. Funerals are generally among the best liturgies in rural Ireland, where we are still spared, for the most part (apart from the homily), the eulogistic excesses that sometimes mar the funeral liturgies in larger urban areas, where secularisation is further advanced. The congregation, being mostly older people and therefore more likely to be regular worshippers, tend to answer the Mass responses better. The filing past the mourners to offer sympathy, and the filling of the grave at the cemetery are rituals in which people, especially men, are not just willing but keen to join.

Baptisms, too, at least in rural Ireland, can be celebrations in which the extended families concerned can be happily and willingly involved. Station Masses, where these survive, or house Masses, can also evoke a similar willingness, while the domestic nature of the setting is more conducive to a feeling of communality among those present.

We generally do 'big' liturgies well – ordinations to the episcopate, priesthood or diaconate, religious professions, church dedications, jubilees of people or of places. The sacramental celebration of 'rites of passage' such as first communion, confirmation and marriage are usually given careful preparation, though one sometimes wonders about the faith content among the people most immediately concerned. One might have a similar concern about some large-scale liturgies organised in second-level schools – an opening of the year Mass or a 'Grad' Mass, in which the vast majority of the attendance is not normally Mass-going and whose link with the church outside of school may be very tenuous. Yet the suggestion that these occasions might be marked with a prayer service rather than a Mass is often not welcomed by school authorities. Many students, of course, might not be aware of the difference, as evidenced by the widespread practice of referring to any kind of religious gathering or group prayer as 'Mass'.

This latter point has come to the fore in recent years in Ireland through the introduction of lay-led liturgies of the Word, which often conclude with the distribution of Holy Communion form the tabernacle. One of the reservations that liturgists have about this is the confusion that can so easily arise between such gatherings and the actual celebration of Mass. This confusion finds expression in statements like 'I really like Tom/Mary Egan's Mass, when the priest is not able to come'. As such liturgies become more common in parishes, greater clarity on this point remains a challenge for catechesis of both adults and children.

The question of liturgical catechesis leads to reflection on the relationship between liturgy and faith. It is sometimes rightly said that good liturgy strengthens faith and bad liturgy weakens it. Perhaps the converse is also true – strong faith expresses itself in good liturgy and weak faith expresses itself in poor liturgy. Do some of the weaknesses in our liturgies have their roots in weakness of faith? And what of the faith of the celebrant? Does he seem conscious of the presence of God to whom he speaks in the Eucharistic Prayer, or does he give the impression of one simply reading (perhaps rather rapidly) words from a book? How does the faith of the celebrant best communicate itself?

More than half a century has now passed since that far-off day in December 1963, when *Sacrosanctum Concilium* was promulgated. In Ireland, as elsewhere, the liturgy that the decree envisaged and as we now celebrate it has become part of the fabric of our Christian lives. Much work has been done and many gains have been achieved in the liturgical life of the Church at home and abroad. There are still areas of concern and issues to be addressed. But overall, as we reflect on what has been achieved, we can make our own the words of the liturgy itself – it is right to give God thanks and praise.

Part IV:
Looking
to the
Future

# CHAPTER 10

## Clergy Morale

THE OPINION is sometimes expressed, both in the media and in conversation among priests, that morale among clergy is at a very low ebb. This is an attempt to reflect on this statement, offering some ideas regarding the factors affecting morale among priests in Ireland at present.

It is difficult to form an accurate impression about the real state of clergy morale in Ireland, since very little research into this area has been carried out. Therefore any generalisation about morale is likely to be quite impressionistic. There is the complicating factor of individual personality styles. Issues such as depression, either endogenous (biologically based) or reactive, as a response to a stressful event or situation (personal bereavement, change of appointment, advancing years, failing health), surely have a bearing on personal morale.

It is interesting to note results described by Fr Stephen Rossetti, in his book *The Joy of Priesthood* (2005), based on a number of surveys done in the US, including some he himself undertook as an aspect of his work in the Saint Luke Institute for clergy in difficulty. These findings included the following: in a survey undertaken by the National Federation of Priests' Councils in the US, in response to a question regarding what priests found to be of 'great importance' as sources of satisfaction; 90% endorsed 'joy of administering the sacraments and leading the liturgy'; 80% endorsed 'preaching the Word'. In a survey conducted by Fr Rossetti himself, 92% of priests endorsed the statement ,'Overall, I feel fulfilled ministering as a priest'; and when given the statement 'I am committed to the ministry of the Catholic Church', 96% said yes. As Fr Rossetti remarks, these are very high rates of commitment and satisfaction, well above the average rate of satisfaction among the general population. In a more recent book, with the striking title, *Why Priests are Happy* (2011), Rossetti confirms these findings. If a similar survey were undertaken in Ireland, the results might be dramatically different or surprisingly similar. Until one is carried out here, we are left with individual impressions.

However, it is undeniable that the self-confidence of clergy has taken a battering in Ireland in recent years. The most obvious factors in this have been: firstly, the revelation of the appalling behaviour of some members of the clergy in relation to children, together with the manner in which these matters were dealt with by some in positions of leadership; and, secondly, the manner in which these revelations were exposed in the media. It is important to make some distinctions here. First, it is appropriate and right that these revelations should affect priests, that they should appal and upset and distress them – not because of the negative light in which they cast the priesthood, but because of the immense damage done to so many vulnerable and innocent children. In so far as the current damage to morale is really a move towards a more realistic and more humble attitude towards our vocation, then it is a salutary and healthy development. With regard to the second aspect of this reality mentioned above, i.e. the manner in which these revelations were exposed and commented on in the media, a further distinction can be made. These exposures, while painful, were a real service to the truth. They exposed a malignant cancer both in the clergy and in the wider society, though this latter aspect seems to get less attention. (At the 'summit' in Rome in February 2019, Pope Francis, and Archbishop Eamon Martin more locally, included this wider context in their words on the subject of abuse.) The media are to be commended for a valuable service to society. However, it must be acknowledged that some of the coverage, and especially some of the comment, as distinct from the reporting, was malicious, vindictive and unfair. It was especially this latter aspect that some clergy found particularly depressing and morale-sapping, particularly as this theme has been returned to again and again over the years. There is also a more general and pervasive anti-Catholic bias in some of the dominant Irish media outlets, and constant exposure to this can have a negative effect on morale.

Another major factor in the lives of Irish priests – and a more long-term and pervasive one – has been the rapid advance of the process of cultural change in Ireland in recent decades, and the corresponding decline in many areas of Church life. We are seeing dwindling and ageing congregations, a sharp drop in vocations to the priesthood, and even more so to the religious or missionary life, the closure of Church institutions and the consequent sale of buildings. In ones pastoral ministry there is also the dispiriting experience of presiding at liturgies – baptisms, first communions, weddings, funerals – which give the impression of having very little faith content, and are becoming to an increasing extent secular rituals or rites of passage. There is also the experience of an ageing and declining presbyterate, and a workload for many that increases as energy diminishes with age.

However, in the face of all these factors, which might seem to impact negatively on morale, it seems that some clergy are better able than others to live happy and fruitful lives, and to engage with present realities in realistic and constructive ways. This raises the more general question of morale in the sense of the factors in the lives of priests that help them to cope more or less successfully with the difficulties that mark, in one way or another, every human life. What are the elements that help us to face life's problems, whether these are common to others – the scandals referred to above, the decline of religious influence in society – or the more individual issues that arise in our personal or pastoral lives? This in turn raises the whole area of human formation, both initial and ongoing, which has assumed such prominence in thinking about the priesthood in recent decades. The basic issue here is how well equipped we are to cope with the human condition in all its complexity.

Observation of colleagues – and, indeed, personal experience –

suggests that the following are some of the important factors that influence the morale of priests and their capacity to live reasonably happy and fulfilled human lives, and to cope well with the times of difficulty of which no human life is totally free.

### Reasonable care of one's physical health

This involves a balanced diet, some regular physical exercise and an adequate amount of rest. The old adage about the healthy mind in a healthy body continues to be true. The housekeeping arrangements of the average priest today can make it easier to slide into carelessness regarding diet, personal appearance and living conditions, and this is not good for morale.

### Healthy nourishment for the mind

We should engage in some good reading, occasional attendance at a good film or play, conversation that engages intelligently with the issues of the day. Tabloid-type reading and dumbed-down TV are the junk food of the mind. A little does no harm, but an undiluted diet leads to mental obesity. Self-discipline regarding TV-watching and the surfing of the Internet is a modern form of asceticism that is needed by priests as well as by anybody wishing to maintain a healthy mind. Online pornography has surfaced as an issue in Ireland, especially among men, and priests are not immune to this. Experts say that addiction to this comes very quickly and easily, even from a couple of initially short or even accidental visits to these sites. Such visits certainly do not enhance morale and may even indicate a serious problem in this area which needs professional help.

### The cultivation and maintenance of a circle of friends

The more variety in the circle – clerical and lay, male and

female – the better. It is important that the circle be reasonably wide, rather than relying excessively on one or two. A good relationship with one's own family – parents, brothers and sisters, nephews and nieces – is also both a good support for morale and a help to being realistic about marriage.

The converse of this may be **the avoidance of certain kinds of company** – cynics, constantly carping critics, pervasively negative people. As Psalm 1 puts it – 'Happy indeed is the man who sits not in the company of scorners … '

### An identity and interests apart from one's ministry

Irish priests in the past have traditionally had a wide range of interests – from farming to football, from gardening to greyhounds, from beekeeping to woodwork, from photography to fishing, from local history to amateur drama, not to mention golf, travel and reading. Provided they don't take over one's life, interests such as these are helpful and wholesome.

### An understanding and acceptance of one's own inner dynamics

Everyone has his own personal history, with its resulting inner compulsions or styles of relating to the world. These can include difficulties, for example with self-esteem, or a latent anger, or a strong desire to please or to control. This is often more obvious to others than it is to ourselves, and colleagues in particular can know the 'buttons to press' that will produce predictable responses. Understanding what 'makes one tick', and compassionately accepting one's inner dynamics makes for a happier life.

### Realistic expectations of oneself and others

A calm and sympathetic understanding of human weakness

– one's own and that of others – saves us from the constant disappointment that comes from excessively high standards that neither we nor those around us can meet.

### A sense of humour

One of the surest signs of good morale is the ability to laugh in a healthy way (a non-cynical, non-bitter way) at our own foibles and those of others. The capacity for not taking ourselves or life around us too terribly seriously is a great blessing.

In addition to these necessary supports for morale, which are common to every human life, there are also a number that are more specific to the priesthood. These include:

### A good relationship with one's parishioners, or those to whom one ministers

It is often commented on that, even at the height of the publicity regarding abuse of children by clergy, people were very supportive of their own priests. People in Ireland still generally have a high regard for the priests whom they know individually, particularly if they have had personal experience of their kindness or pastoral care. Where this is the case, it contributes significantly to personal morale.

### A good relationship with one's bishop

A sense that one is known and appreciated by him as a person, a colleague and friend, and not just as a unit of pastoral productivity. The smaller the diocese the easier this is to achieve. Some bishops are naturally better than others at affirming and supporting priests, and all of them now operate with the extra stresses placed on the priest-bishop relationship by necessary child-protection policies. It is worth noting that bishops themselves are also in need of affirmation and support, just as much as any other priests, or perhaps even more so.

### An ability to let go of the past

Particularly of the specific form of church life as those of us of a certain age experienced it in the middle decades of the last century, with its extraordinarily high level of religious practice, and the superabundance of clergy and the high status they enjoyed in society. One factor in low morale may be a kind of grieving for the passing of all of that, and may be a stage we need to go through in moving to a new situation.

### A wide historical view of the life of the Church, as well as a broad geographical perspective

Historically, the Church, both universally and in Ireland, has gone through a great variety of modes of being present in society. There may be a sub-conscious tendency to view the Irish Church of the 1950s as a kind of optimal model, one against which our present experience is measured and found wanting. But it was only one model, and for all its positive and negative features, it has now passed into history and we are moving towards something new.

Geographically, the centre of the Church's gravity, both in terms of numbers and of vitality, is clearly moving to the southern hemisphere. Europe is seen as the most problematic continent for the Church at present, the one where the process of secularisation has moved furthest and deepest. For good or ill, we are Europeans, and it is in this context that we are called to live our Christian faith and our priesthood. Being aware of this reality, accepting what we cannot change about it, and **being able to search for the**

**best possible way to be present as communities of faith in contemporary Europe**, are important for our personal and group morale.

## The cultivation and nourishment of our personal faith by means of a sustained and strong prayer life

The final, and perhaps most fundamental, element in the personal morale of priests. Without this, we can become ecclesiastical functionaries, working for a not particularly successful branch of a multinational organisation called the Catholic Church. Only faith gives sense and meaning to how we live our lives, and faith of the depth needed for the wholesome and happy living of the priesthood can only be sustained by a strong and committed prayer life. Prayer, if it is really authentic, integrates spirituality with our humanity. Elements such as spiritual reading and spiritual direction can nourish a genuine prayer life. Regular thoughtful celebration, as a penitent, of the sacrament of reconciliation can help us to find reassurance and encouragement for our personal and pastoral journey. Practices such as the 'examen of consciousness' can help us to find God in the sometimes messy bits and pieces of our human lives. Prayer on its own, of course, will not ensure a good personal morale unless it is supported by some combination of the other elements mentioned previously. Grace must build on nature, but without faith sustained by prayer, it is difficult to see how the priesthood makes any kind of sense. If a life does not make sense, it is very difficult to see how it can be lived with that combination of commitment, enthusiasm, contentment and fulfilment that we mean when we use the word 'morale'.

# CHAPTER 11

## A New Evangelisation

Throughout the papacy of Pope John Paul II, we frequently heard him speak of 'a new evangelisation', and some of us, at least, wondered exactly what that might be. Pope Benedict further heightened the profile of this idea, firstly by creating a new office in Rome to address the issue and then by proposing the idea as the theme for the 2012 Synod of Bishops. How might one try to articulate what a 'new evangelisation' might involve in an Irish context, particularly from the viewpoint of parish pastoral life?

In a general sense, the idea of a new evangelisation seems to emerge from situations where the effects of the original proclamation of the Gospel, and the local churches that emerged from that, have grown weak in faith – for example in the secularised Western world, especially in Europe. In these situations, there is a felt need to renew the vitality of faith communities weakened by a great variety of factors – sociological change, urbanisation, the rise of extreme individualism, the effects of the mass media on popular consciousness, the tendency to privatise religion and remove it from the public sphere.

It is clear to observers of the Irish scene that the process that created the present religious situation for Christianity in mainland Europe was slower to arrive in Ireland, but that we have more or less 'caught up' with Europe, as evidenced by the rapidity and depth of the change we have seen in almost all aspects of Irish life in recent decades, not least in the religious sphere. There are factors that are peculiar to Ireland, too – the historically close relationship between Catholicism and Irish nationalism, the majoritarian position of the Catholic Church, and indeed its dominance, which some would see as a domineering presence – in so many aspects of Irish life, particularly in the Irish Republic in the half century or so after the achievement of independence. Something of a reaction against that perceived dominance is certainly part of the Irish religious landscape at present. There is also the impact of scandal on the life of the Church in Ireland – as elsewhere – which has hastened the decline in adherence to the Church.

Church adherence has been and still is the main feature of the faith of the Irish people. When we use the word 'faith' in the Irish context, what we mean is not mainly acceptance of revealed truth or personal commitment to Christ and to his message, but mostly a sense of belonging to, or being part of a community with certain beliefs, traditions and rituals, and a greater or lesser degree of willingness to engage with these traditions and rituals, especially the Mass. It could be described as an ecclesiocentric more than a Christocentric form of faith. Of course, the whole purpose of the Church's existence is to lead people into relationship with Christ, but the extent to which that happens, or ever happened in Ireland is debatable. Belonging, turning up and being there were regarded as being of primary importance. The purpose of the gathering and of the gathered community – to hear and welcome the word of God, to express and deepen relationship to Christ and commitment to the values and vision he taught – seemed secondary, at least in the popular awareness, if not in the minds of the leaders.

There are those who claim that some Irish people may in fact be 'practical atheists' – they do not deny the existence of God, any more than they deny the existence of the planet Jupiter, but both are equally remote and irrelevant to everyday life. They live their lives as if God did not exist, except as a kind of last resort at times of major crises or difficulties in their lives. Pope Benedict wrote and spoke a lot along these lines, not specifically about Ireland, but his words are applicable here too.

The Catholic faith sometimes seems like a veil that lies lightly over the lives of most of our parishioners – the provider of rituals to mark stages and moments in their lives – a source, among others, to which they may look to for answers to life's deeper questions whenever these occur to them, which may well be seldom – a kind of general, rather vague framework for life. As regards attitudes and lifestyles, these come not so much from faith sources as from the general culture around them – this general culture is filtered through family, school, peer group and friends, and by the media, especially TV and social media. Attitudes and opinions, generally without much reflection or deliberate choice, come from these sources.

It is clear that Ireland is in at least as much need of a new evangelisation as any other country in the Western world. In thinking about what this might involve, we need to ask ourselves what are the positive signs in the Irish religious landscape and where are the possible entry points for a new sharing of the Gospel. One element immediately suggests itself – the continuing attachment of the Irish people to the rituals of Catholicism. The great majority of Irish people still wish to have their children baptised, to receive their first communion and to be confirmed. Most families still want a Christian funeral for their departed members. It is tempting to be largely negative in our assessment of the religious significance of these rites of passage, seeing them as mostly secular celebrations with at best a thin veneer of religious belief, and little or no religious commitment accompanying them. Yet for all these negative features, there is still a possible entry point in these occasions, of which the new evangelisation might make use, given a new approach and a new attitude towards people wishing to mark family and personal milestones with these rituals. This will involve moving away from any negativity or cynicism or even annoyance and impatience with people, and a move towards a new attitude and a new kind of approach that is able to make sharing in the life of the Church, and access to the message and person of Jesus, attractive and inviting.

The new evangelisation is not first of all about new methods or strategies. It is largely about new attitudes, particularly towards those we wish to evangelise. These attitudes include, much more than heretofore, a deep respect for the human dignity of each person, no matter how offputting his or her manner and lifestyle and apparent religious indifference may be. It involves a more serious attempt to understand the person and the factors and influences that make his or her religious situation so different from mine and from how I think he or she should be. In the end, it's about love in the best sense of that word. We cannot evangelise anyone unless in some sense, we love them first, and love involves respect, acceptance, an attempt to understand, good will and a wish for the growth and good of the other. The word 'evangelisation' is often taken to mean proclamation of one kind or another, a transmission or communication of the Gospel message. But in order for this to happen, a relationship must first be established between the proclaimer and those to whom the message is addressed. This is why warmth and welcome, respect, acceptance and understanding are necessary before the message can be heard by those for whom it is destined. It is elementary in 'foreign' missionary methodology to study closely the culture of those whom one wishes to evangelise, and to communicate first of all to them a deep respect for all that is positive in their lives, religious traditions and communities. Any new evangelisation will need to do this too.

Pope Saint Paul VI, in an oft-quoted phrase, said that the people of today listen more to witnesses than to teachers, and if they listen to teachers it is because they are witnesses. To expand on this idea, one might say that those who wish to share the Gospel must somehow incarnate it in their own lives and personalities. They must mirror something of the attractiveness of Christ. What was it that drew people to Jesus of Nazareth? Was it his compassion, his mercy, his understanding, his kindness, his joy, his patience? It was surely all of these and much more besides. Somehow, he communicated love to them, and they sensed in him the presence of the ultimate source of all love, the one whom he addressed as Abba, Father. Christ-like people who, by a combination of the gifts of nature and grace, can reproduce something of that in their own lives and in their manner of relation to others will surely make the best evangelisers.

All this implies that those who wish to share the Gospel message must be deeply steeped in that message themselves. All who wish to bring Christ into the lives of others must first have welcomed him wholeheartedly into their own lives. They must be people of personal holiness. All of this suggests a deep and sustained personal prayer life, the lifelong effort to let the message that Jesus came to bring (and to be) soak its way more and more deeply into the deepest recesses of the heart. Pope Francis has written about what this means in practice in *Gaudete et Exsultate*, and the fact that so many people find the personality of Pope Francis so attractive and appealing suggests that he is one good model of what an evangeliser might be like, one who tries to practise what he preaches.

All of this holds true at the level of Christian communities as well as in the lives of individuals. People are attracted to faith by the quality of authentic Christian community life as they encounter it. People are drawn towards any kind of community, large or small, where the fruits of the Spirit mark the interactions of the people of that community – love, joy, peace, patience, kindness, gentleness, faithfulness, self-control. We are told that those who observed the life of the earliest Christian communities said, 'See how these Christians love one another.' That was surely evangelisation by witness, and the challenge to our communities – neighbourhoods, parishes, dioceses, church organisations and movements – is to share the Gospel message by that kind of witness in our time.

There is one particular strand of thought on Christian community that merits some consideration. It is described by the phrase 'the Benedict option'. The inspiration for this way of thinking comes from reflection on the life and influence of St Benedict of Nursia, generally regarded as the father of Western monasticism. He lived at a time when the Roman Empire was in a state of decay and collapse and chaos, as violence and moral decadence engulfed most of Europe. Benedict's response was to create small oases of peace and order and lifestyles ruled by faith. These oases were the first Benedictine monasteries, and in them was preserved something of Roman civilisation when it was at its best, grafted onto the Christian faith especially by means of a monastic rule. As the centuries passed, the monasteries become a powerful source of a renewal, both of the Church and of civil society. The Benedict option suggests that something similar is needed in our day – that our civilisation is on a road to decay and eventual collapse, in many ways comparable to the chaos of the Dark Ages, and that Christians should withdraw into counter-cultural oases in order to protect and defend fundamental human and Christian values that are being lost in contemporary society.

There is some merit and validity in this way of thinking, but some danger also. The danger is that if Christians withdraw too far from the world, they become something like a sect or even a cult, a group of like-minded people, with very fixed views, marked by hostility to the 'outside' world, and vulnerable to unhealthy forms of manipulative leadership. The validity of this option is that it provides a support for a faith-based understanding and living of life that is unlikely to find such support elsewhere. The challenge is to keep these two elements in balance and in dialogue – to be counter-cultural without being anti-cultural, to realise that we are not situated outside the culture, judging it, but within the culture trying to be a positive presence there. Our call is to be faithful to values and principles without being condemnatory of other views, to be engaged with the world without being dominated by it. This is a difficult balance to keep, but essential if a group is to be authentically Christian.

In *Evangelii Gaudium*, the foundational document of his papacy, Pope Francis explores the theme of evangelisation extensively. One of his central themes is the role of the Holy Spirit as the primary agent in the mission of sharing the Gospel message of Jesus. The call of Christians is to be open to the Spirit, to discern the call of God for the Church in all the forms of its presence, local and worldwide. Our call here in Ireland must surely be to attune the ears of our hearts and souls to what the voice of God is saying to us now in the Ireland of today, so that we may discover or rediscover the joy of the Gospel.